Name Reality

by

Lyon G. Payley Zonamyari

to my dear frend Gill
with love & gratitude

TELEMACHUS PRESS

NAME REALITY

Cover designed by Lyon G. Payley Zonamyari

Cover art:
Copyright © 23069784/iStock

Published by Telemachus Press, LLC
http://www.telemachuspress.com

Visit the author website:
http://www.namesdoctor.com

ISBN: 978-1-939927-73-6 (eBook)
ISBN: 978-1-939927-74-3 (Paperback)

Version 2013.11.2

Printed in the United States of America

10 9 8 7 6 5 4 3 2 1

TABLE OF CONTENTS

Foreword

by Dr. Tito Palacio

Throughout my professional years as a medical and homeopathic doctor, I have always known our names produce a vibration that reflects upon the conditions of our bodies. Until now, I have not been able to connect the two together, especially for patient diagnosis. The system Lyon has shown to me and demonstrated with the voluntary consent of my patients is conclusive evidence that the connection exists.

Lyon was able to confirm medical issues that matched my diagnosis. In some cases, he added more information that was beneficial to both me and the patient.

Lyon correctly quotes in his book; when conventional methods have failed to diagnose or cure a problem, this book provides the missing link.

I can conclude by saying, I do not see any reason why this system should not be used as an additional tool to help discover, prevent, combat or aid recovery with many physical and mental ailments.

Dr. Tito Palacio.

Name Reality

Introduction

WHAT DOES YOUR NAME SAY ABOUT YOU

Name (***meaning, a word that constitutes the distinctive designation of a person***)
Reality (***meaning, in truth, the here and now, the totality of real things and events***)

Name Reality is a documented hermeneutical system that shows who you really are and why life has not always gone the way you planned. *Name Reality* shows why some of us appear to lead happy stress free lives and others do not. *Name Reality* shows why some years you try so hard but cannot get ahead. What makes one person a brilliant scholar yet another becomes a drop out? This incredible system can be your turning point if you want to understand yourself better, need to improve specific areas of your life, or want to create a new vibrant, healthy, successful, happy name for you or your baby.

Name Reality reveals how, from birth, your documented names shape and define your character, your personality, both your mental and physical health, for better or worse. More amazing, the letters from each of your names rotate at predetermined years, influencing the way you live your life. Your names can bring you success or failure, influence love, health and happiness. Parents can unknowingly name their kids with a life of bliss, fame and fortune or sickness, doom and gloom. One letter can make a huge difference. Ana. Ann. Anna. Anne. *Name Reality* shows you which name balances best with your family name.

The combination of your names can be likened to a dress or suit, an outfit that you wear for life. It makes a statement. It says who you are and can influence the way other people see you. Your names, like your clothes, need balance. A great outfit can be ruined by the wrong pair of shoes or a goofy hat. Each letter in your name emits a frequency, like the keys on a piano. Play the right combination of notes and you have beautiful music. Play the wrong combination of notes and at best you are out of tune, or worst, you become a dreadful noise.

So why has nobody told you this before? If you have read anything about the *laws of attraction*, you will know it was a secret knowledge kept hidden from the public, known only to a few privileged families. Analyzing names, another fundamental principal action of the Universe, was also kept under lock and key for centuries. It was lost then found, swept aside and now again, rediscovered.

WHERE DOES THIS SYSTEM ORIGINATE FROM

Analyzing names can be traced back several thousand years. This knowledge was originally known and used, solely by the elite families of Egypt, the Chaldea and Hebrew Countries in the Middle East.

On the day a child was born to one of these families, an astrological chart was calculated, then, using this analysis system, a name was created for the baby specifically to improve the qualities of that child's life. More recently, some 3000 years ago, this system found its way to China.

It was in China that this knowledge was recorded and preserved in its splendid entirety, known to the ancients as "The Way of Life". A much more complicated version can be found in the Indian Vedas and in the Hebrew Cabbalas. Discovered in Egypt, the great hieratic papyrus known as the "Book of the Master of the Secret House" was preserved at the library of the Louvre in Paris. A copy was translated and published by W. Marsham Adams.

In 1929, a compilation of all these scripts was written and published by Veolita Parke Boyle. Titled; "The Fundamental Principles of Yi-King

Tao, the Cabbalas of Egypt and the Hebrews". Both Veolita and her sister Elvrita, devoted their lives to the study of names, based on the Chinese "Sacred Science of Vibration". Unfortunately, back then, almost a century ago, her book received little recognition. People were a long way from the New Age and many regarded her book as nothing more than superstition.

Veolita presented her work to Professor William H. Hallock from the department of physics, Colombia University in the USA. He acknowledged that the study showed numbers and letters call into action certain forces present in the vibratory waves of the universe and these forces do react upon our bodies affecting the conditions of our lives. He went on to quote; "If you have made as much investigation as this and found it answers to that number of tests, then the force is *there* and has *got* to be reckoned with."

Music shows how different vibrations, created by one or another style, be it rock and pop or county and classical, affects our bodies. Even non-aficionados cannot resist moving or reacting when, a rhythm or beat strikes a sound in tune with your own vibration. Some people become so excited they feel the need to sing along or get up and dance. One song can make you incredibly happy and another song will bring you to tears. It is no wonder that music is such a huge industry. If one song doesn't get to you, another one will.

UNDERSTANDING THIS INCREDIBLE SYSTEM CAN TRANSFORM YOUR LIFE

About 25 years ago, Veolita's interpretations were studied and expanded by a gentleman in England named Laurence Payg. I was introduced to Laurence in 2010. So impressed by this incredible system, I decided to learn more, first through Laurence and then by obtaining a copy of Veolita's book. After three years and countless hours of study, I decided to use the longer but more detailed method to analyze names as described by Veolita in her book. My book, *Name Reality*, gives you an easy to read updated view of how the system works. It gives you the opportunity to analyze your own name, other people's names and how to create new names, with simple step by step instructions.

OTHER NAME STUDIES

There are hundreds of books and websites that offer the historic or religious meaning of names. Some give relevant information towards one name, but most are limited and none offer useful ways to interpret the combined meaning of all your names. Two people with the same first or last name will have something in common, but it ends there at something. *Name Reality* reveals so much more.

This system is so incredibly accurate you can virtually disregard everything else written about the understanding and meaning of names. At first glance, *Name Reality* may appear very similar to numerology. However, this is not the case. Numerology is a good system, but *Name Reality* is very different and probes way deeper. *Name Reality* shows how you are the unique blend of all your names and goes further by explaining how individual letters from your names affect events for each and every year of your life. *Name Reality Analysis* is the only system that enables you to accurately modify, change or create a name to a specific personality and create positive or negative events at predetermined years.

NAME REALITY IS LIKE SHEET MUSIC

Name Reality is a mathematical system relating the vibration of each letter in your name to a number. Your combined letters produce your name. Similar as the keys on a piano are related to notes and the combination of notes produce a chord.

The sound of music produced by a piano can be documented with sheet music. The vibration produced by your names can be documented with *Name Reality.*

Name Reality shows how each of the names you have indicate your character, your personality, both your mental and physical health, for better or worse. You are the combination of all your names.

Name Reality then goes further to show how the letters in each of your names, influence events which will occur at specific times during your life.

This shows you when the positive years in your life commence, allowing you to take advantage. It also shows you when negative events or difficult years begin, allowing you time to prepare or make advance plans.

This system helps you to know where and when to focus your time, your effort and resources to obtain maximum results. This system will not tell you which lottery numbers to play. However it will give you an accurate *weather forecast*. Knowing which year to carry an umbrella or take your sun glasses, will enhance the quality of your life.

Preparing a *Name Reality Analysis* for yourself or someone who is important to you, can be rewarding and life changing.

Creating a positive name for a newborn can be a wonderful gift for life.

NAME CHANGE CAN ALTER YOUR LIFE

Two examples where changing your name can alter your life is evident in the world of entertainment and marriage. Movie stars and pop musicians are a good example of what can happen when you change your name. How many have struggled to achieve fame, until they chose the right name. Were they less talented before choosing their new name? I doubt it!

In many countries, women take the family name of their husbands upon marriage. Sometimes, the new name can blend well and improve life for the better. Unfortunately, it can also have the opposite effect. How often have you heard of couples living together, happy for many years, but who break up soon after marriage? *Name Reality* shows how, in many cases, it was the name change that altered the dynamics for the worse. Statistics show the divorce rate in Europe and the USA is around 50%. Yet in South America and Latin America, where women do not take the family name of their husbands, divorce rate is 5%.

NAME REALITY IS THE MISSING LINK

There are hundreds of renowned and respected self-help gurus. Many have written or produced excellent books. They mostly point in the same direction. Positive Speaking with Positive Thinking reinforced by Positive Visualization will improve your life. Books like "*The Secret*" by Rhonda Byrne, gained huge worldwide attention. Best sellers like "*The Richest Man Who Ever Lived*" by Steven K Scott takes a more religious approach by relating to the biblical Book of Proverbs. My favorite is a book that was first published in 1963. *The Power Of Your Subconscious Mind*, by Dr. Joseph Murphy, more recently revised by Dr. Ian McMahan. Many people have gained from these books, yet many have failed so abysmally. Why?

If you have names with negative tendencies leaning towards anger, anxiety, doubt, hesitation, fears or phobias, this will most surely restrict your potential and slow or even stop your progress. If you have negative letter combinations in your events chart, it will delay or block your advancement during the years those letters are working against you. The more negatives you have, the more difficult it is to get ahead. If you have tried self-help methods and failed, it was probably not for lack of trying. It is most likely your names, or the letter combinations you were in at that time, prevented you from reaching your goals.

TAKE CONTROL OF YOUR LIFE

When you understand all your names, if a negative part of your personality or certain letters bring negative events into your life, you can make advance plans. You can change, overcome or reduce these potential problems. Self-awareness and understanding oneself, is sometimes enough to enable you to make the necessary corrections, with positive attitude and positive visualization. Some people may not feel the need to change their name at all. It is your free choice.

CHANGE YOUR NAME

You cannot change your date, time and place of birth, thus changing your astrological chart. However, one of the very few things you can change about yourself is your name. Changing your name will change your vibration, which can turn your life around for the better. Sometimes changing just one name, the way you spell a name, or adding middle initials, can make a huge difference.

Like a new custom made designer dress or suit, it will change the way you feel about yourself and the way other people see you. The shoes will fit and the hat will add style. Doors will begin to open, improving your life, with love, health and happiness. Your piano will play the right combination of keys producing beautiful music to be heard by you and the people who surround you.

My research shows when you commit to changing your name, effects begin immediately and increase with every document you change. The more you want it, the faster it happens. I have witnessed some people experience a rapid transformation with their life quickly taking a new direction, becoming calm, more focused and more positive in the way they think and speak. A balanced name with positive letters has no obstacles and sets you free. Self-help techniques will begin to work, bringing out the positive qualities in your astrological chart. You will grow and develop, taking better control of both your life and your future.

Part One
Your personal guide to understanding names.

Chapter One

JIBBA JABBA MYTH

I am sure you are curious but thinking is this some hokey pokey jibba jabba myth? You may ask: who created this system? How does it work and does it even work at all? Let's keep it simple, take your choice of these two options.

Option 1/. *Name Reality* works. Yes, it really works. Try it for yourself and you will see. Microwave ovens work. Most of us have no clue how they cook the things you put inside but we know they work. Electricity, radio, television and Internet, they all work. Do you question it? No. We take it for granted and use these things in everyday life. Just like following the instructions when using any of the above devices for the first time, do the same with your names. You will see that it too, works very well.

Option 2/. This entire planet is made up from one thing, energy. *Energy is vibration.* There is no difference between water, ice and a pan of boiling water producing steam. It is the same water, just at different vibrations. We humans, like everything on this planet, have different vibrations making up our skin, bones and yes, our names. This book will show you the different vibrations created by letters of the alphabet and how they affect both our personality and our day-to-day lives.

Who discovered it? Who invented it? Well, we can go back about 10,000 years to find scraps of information. There are documented Masonic links, so maybe there is a connection with the Illuminati dating way back and beyond. We know they knew about the system and we know they kept it a secret. But really, we are back to the pyramid theories. Nobody really knows for sure. All we can assume is that it came from intelligence far greater than we know today. We know with modern GPS that the pyramids and other creations like Stonehenge are positioned exactly within millimeters to one another in a formation related to each other or points within the Universe. We know that the massive blocks used to build the pyramids that interlock so precisely were not cut by hand or machine. Either some outside assistance was there or man had unknown technologies in use at that time. There are many questions about the history and even the existence of the planet on which we live. Crop circles still baffle scientists. It is doubtful we will find conclusive evidence anytime soon. So ....

You might want to go with option one.

Simply try it and see. I did and it works very well!

My life, though far from tragic, was a rollercoaster ride with constant unexplainable ups and downs. I came from a stable middle class family. I was a grade A student and sports athlete of the year before becoming a drop out in my early teens.

I always worked for myself, which financially made matters worse. Had I been employed, I might have simply lost my job. However, being self-employed and running my own business, I went bankrupt, no less than three times.

The first time was at the young age of twenty-four. Later, when the recession hit in the late 1980's, I was riding high. My competitors were failing and I was succeeding. I was good at what I did, but I can remember at the time thinking, why am I doing so well? I sold my business at the end of 1991 and I took a year off. Early in 1993, I tried to get back into business. Every venture I tried for the next three years failed abysmally. However, as usual, I bounced back. The next eleven years I was riding high once again, and then, yes, you guessed it, back down to nothing. People who knew my capability and devotion to my work could not understand why. I too could not understand why?

Outside of work, my personal life was also a roller coaster. Looking back, there are many times I can reflect and say I was a total ass. I was unpredictable, caring one day, yet selfish and dishonest the next. I was usually very extroverted, but sometimes very introverted. I began drinking heavily as a teenager. In my mind, I was a "social drinker". I would work hard by day and drink hard by night. Like most people, I truly believed I was normal. We all think it is the other guy who needs a shrink, until the *reality* sinks in.

In 2010, I was looking for answers. My daughter told me of a man in England who analyzes people names. Desperate, I thought I had nothing to lose. Sure enough, some of my troubles were revealed. Reading the events in my life created by the revolving letters from each of my names was a slam-dunk. My first name then was Paul. The letter U represents loss. It lasts for three years. Sure enough, every bankruptcy was timed exactly to the re-occurrence of this letter. I had three years of loss followed by eleven years of power success and advancement influenced by the P, A and L. At first, I was not totally convinced by the readings for my personality, but this was due to the fact I was still in denial. On reflection, the readings were mostly accurate.

Like a microwave oven, this analysis process works, and it works *very well.*

In my introduction, I likened both names and letters to the keys on a piano. If you want to know what tune you play, piano lessons start in the next chapter.

Chapter Two

LET'S GET STARTED

This is now it works. There are 64 personality types dividing the human race, just as there are 64 fundamental forces that constitute the action of the Universe. You may have seen the numbers 1 to 64 before, from the I Ching to the number of squares on a chess-board. It is recognized as a powerful mathematical force. Do not confuse *Name Reality* with numerology. *The two are not the same.* In *Name Reality*, numbers are selected for each letter in your name, then added together to calculate which of the 64 personality types you have for each one of your names. Each name has two personalities. I call these *primary* and *undertone.* Each name you have is the result of both these personalities. In turn, you are the combination of the personalities from all of your names. This goes further to include your mother's maiden name and the date of the day you were born. Every one of us is the combination of at least 7 personalities or 9 if you have a middle name.

You can see how by a quick mathematical calculation you are one in 500 million or one in 200 billion if you have a middle name. Like the odds of two people having the same fingerprints or DNA. *This system is incredibly accurate.*

There are a few people in England who practice the basics of this system, but they only use one personality per name and do not include mother's maiden name or day of birth. This is fine if you want a quick overview. However, I must stress this will obviously leave you short changed missing many important details about yourself. This is similar to comparing a birth sign reading from a magazine to a full professional astrological chart.

When creating a new name, you must include all names for evaluation. You must calculate not only the primary, but also the undertone personalities and the birth date.

The second part of *Name Reality* reveals how letters in your names change and rotate on your birthday, which influences events each and every year of your life. Every letter has a definition. Some are good, some are not so good. Again, it is the combination of these three or four letters, one from each of your names that dictate influences for that year of your life. For example; F, H, U, V, W and X usually have a negative influence. C, G, J, K, L, N, P, Q, Y and Z have a positive influence. Letters A, B, D, E, I, M O, R, S and T can swing either way depending upon the positive or negative from other letters in the table for that same year.

Here are a few guidelines you need to know before analyzing your name:

It is very important you use your documented legal name in full. For example, take John Michael Smith. His mother's maiden name was Jones and he was born on the 15th. You analyze John Michael Smith Jones and personality number 15 for his day of birth.

Nicknames do not have much bearing except in cases where the name used is heavily publicized and documented. Take Michael Andrew (J) Fox, the star of the "Back to the future" movies in the 1980's. He willingly created the initial J because he did not want to be referred to as Michael A. Fox, hence Michael J. Fox. Everybody knows him as Michael J. Fox, everybody calls him Michael J. Fox and the name has been blasted in bold print worldwide. The J has an effect on his personality and life events from the day he added this letter to his names. From birth we analyze

Michael Andrew Fox (Piper), his mother's maiden name and 9 for his date of birth. Later we add the J into his combination of names.

Another good example as to when a name should or should not be included for calculation would be my dear friend Kate from London. Her birth certificate and name from birth was Catherine. Her personality and events throughout her early years read as Catherine despite many people calling her Kate, which was her name of choice. When she was nineteen years old, she applied for her first passport. At that time, computer systems were not commercially used.

She applied for her passport with the name Kate and without question that was what they gave her. Subsequently, her driver's license went the same way and her first bank account too. It did not take long before all her documents except her birth certificate used the name Kate. Working closely together, we established she had changed her life at that precise time by combining a process of desire, free will, and most importantly, documentation. Prior to age nineteen, despite many years of calling herself Kate, she was for *Name Reality* purposes, Catherine. After age nineteen, we add the name Kate to her birth names.

In the words of the late great Sir Winston Churchill, *"you create your own Universe as you go along"*.

Hyphenated or double barreled names are not considered one word. They are calculated as two individual names. Titles, Sir, Lord, Doctor, Captain, Sr. or Jr. do not come into the calculation, so disregard them. Ignore Le, La, De, Des, De la, Van and Van de. However Mc, Mac, D' as in D'Arcy or O as in O'Connor are included within the name.

Name change for women by marriage follows a similar path as the example of Kate. You do not delete your maiden name for calculation purposes unless you specifically stated the request in writing on a legal document at any time or by making a legal name change.

Mary Jo Anderson born on the 15th whose mother's maiden name was Smith, married Michael Jones in 2007. You analyze Mary Jo Anderson Smith 15 before 2007 and Mary Jo Anderson Smith 15 Jones after 2007.

Divorce alone does not take away a name you gained through marriage. You must legally renounce your married name and revert back to your maiden name. This process is more common in the USA where women frequently choose to revert back to their original names on driver's licenses, passports and other important documents. This logically makes sense! If the marriage didn't work, why would you want to keep his name!

If Mary divorced in 2009 and remarried in 2010 without legally renouncing her previous married name, she carries the divorced name. When she later married John Brown in 2010, poor Mary becomes Mary Jo Anderson Smith 15 Jones Brown. As you can imagine, this invariably becomes a tangled mess. It also becomes a more difficult task to analyze with so many names producing so many variables.

I have a good friend who was in this predicament. She has been married three times in the last forty years. Finally, she has great husband and a very nice life, yet she is going through stressful times. We identified the reasons by unraveling both the names and the long combination of letters in her events chart.

Adoption is considered a legal name change. You delete or erase your old name and take the new name from the day the papers are signed. Your original birth name becomes just a memory and the changes begin. Your personality will change to the new combination of names. The events in your life will follow the pattern generated by the new names. If a child is adopted at age three, the original birth names and chart will remain in effect up until that time. The new chart will begin from the legal day of the name change.

The following chapters will show you how to calculate names, how they shape and define your character and the way letters from each of your names influence your day-to-day life. The chapters in part two, go into more detail about balance. This will be of most interest to those searching for the answers to why life has not gone the way they had hoped and planned.

Bon voyage!

Chapter Three

CONVERT NAMES TO NUMBERS

This is the part where *Name Reality* can sometimes be confused with numerology. The only connection to numerology is the mathematical use of numbers, one to nine for letters A to Z and the 64 personalities that can be reduced to a single digit. *Name Reality* and numerology are very different and have no other similarities.

Reducing numbers has been well documented for thousands of years. Cabbalistic reduction, as it is known, dates way back in Masonic history. It is believed to have been used by the great philosopher and mathematician Pythagorus. It was taught to Moses. He passed it on and it has been used by every Hebrew Cabbalist since.

This is how it works; *If mathematics is not your strong subject, do not worry. You can forgo this part and go to the next page where the letters A to Z have been conveniently converted to numbers for you.*

There are 26 letters of the alphabet from A to Z. The letter A is given the number 1. The letter B is given the number 2. C is 3, D is 4 and so on. The letter I is 9. When we get to J, you would be correct to assume it is 10. However, we reduce it to a single digit by adding the two original digits together. 1 plus 0 is 1, so J is given the number 1. K is 11, so 1 + 1 is 2. The letter L is 12, so 1 plus 2 is 3, and so on.

Here is a list of numbers from 10 to 26 so you can clearly see the reduction of all numbers applicable to the alphabet. The same principle will apply later when you are looking at the 64 different personalities. 6 plus 4 is 10 and 1 plus 0 is 1. Therefore, 64 becomes a 1. When you have a name like Christopher, which totals 67, there is no personality number 67, so you have to reduce the 67 one time. Add 6 and 7 to produce 13 and analyze this number. In turn, 4 will be the reduced number for 13.

10 is 1, 11 is 2, 12 is 3, 13 is 4, 14 is 5, 15 is 6, 16 is 7, 17 is 8 and 18 is 9.

19 is 1 plus 9 = 10. Then 1 + 0 is 1.

20 is 2, 21 is 3, 22 is 4, 23 is 5, 24 is 6, 25 is 7 and 26 is 8.

You will see A, J, S have the value of one. B, K, T is two, and so on.

Primary Numbers Chart

1	2	3	4	5	6	7	8	9
A	B	C	D	E	F	G	H	I
J	K	L	M	N	O	P	Q	R
S	T	U	V	W	X	Y	Z	#

Using this system, let's convert some names to number. Try John Michael Smith born on the 25th whose mother's maiden name was Jones. Write the appropriate number under each letter of the name. Then below that add the individual numbers together and write the total for each name.

J	O	H	N		M	I	C	H	A	E	L		S	M	I	T	H		J	O	N	E	S		25
1	6	8	5		4	9	3	8	1	5	3		1	4	9	2	8		1	6	5	5	1		25
20					33								24						18						25

What is important to understand next are undertone numbers. You may recall earlier in the book I mentioned how every name is made up from 2 personalities. I call these primary and undertone. Primary are the numbers above you calculated for John Michael Smith Jones. Undertones are another set of numbers that are literally for a better word, *underlying* personality traits. How much of these underlying personality traits show, can vary from person to person. First, I will show you how to calculate these undertone numbers. Then I will discuss more on how to read these numbers in the chapters that follow.

Remember, this chapter is titled how to convert names to numbers. You must get this first step right. One letter or one number calculated incorrectly can completely change the reading for your name. Double check your additions.

Undertone numbers use the same Cabbalistic reduction process but by flipping everything upside down. I will explain this process but again, if the number calculations become a little confusing, I have supplied an easy to read chart you can refer to on the next page.

To calculate undertone numbers you start with the original primary number, for example 5. The principle is to add a number to the primary number, in this case 5, to make it add up to a 9, so, 5 plus 4 = 9. Therefore, the undertone number of 5 is 4. The exception is 9, which cannot change from a 9.

1 becomes 8, 2 become 7, 3 becomes 6, 4 becomes 5, 5 becomes 4, 6 becomes 3, 7 becomes 2, 8 becomes 1 and 9 is always 9. You can make this process of addition to calculate undertone name numbers or simply use the undertone A to Z chart I have prepared for you.

One exception to the rule on undertones is your birth day. There is no undertone number for your birth day. The number of the day you are born is that number.

Undertone Numbers Chart

9	8	7	6	5	4	3	2	1
#	A	B	C	D	E	F	G	H
I	J	K	L	M	N	O	P	Q
R	S	T	U	V	W	X	Y	Z

Now make another set of numbers for John Smith. Write the appropriate number under each letter of the name. Then below that write the total for each name.

J	O	H	N		M	I	C	H	A	E	L		S	M	I	T	H		J	O	N	E	S		25
8	3	1	4		5	9	6	1	8	4	6		8	5	9	7	1		8	3	4	4	8		25
16					39								30						27						25

The final set of numbers you need will look like this. (primary/undertone)

J	O	H	N		M	I	C	H	A	E	L		S	M	I	T	H		J	O	N	E	S		25
20/16					33/39								24/30						18/27						25

To analyze the name of John Michael Smith Jones born on the 25th you read the personality pages for numbers 20, 16, 33, 39, 24, 30, 18, 27 and 55. This may seem a daunting task. It is not if you follow the instructions in the next chapters. Please do calculate the numbers for your names now. Avoid temptation to read the name definitions until you have read further on. First read Chapter Four—*Undertones*, Chapter Five—*Don't shoot me I am only the messenger* and Chapter Six—*How to read your name.*

In the words of Forrest Gump, *"life is like a box of chocolates. You never know what ya gonna get"*. To avoid a bad taste in your mouth, read all the instructions first.

If you want speed and accuracy for calculating multiple numbers of names both primary and undertone together with a lifetime events chart, I have a program you can download to your computer available through my website.

www.namesdoctor.com

Chapter Four

UNDERTONES

The previous chapter introduced the word undertone and showed how to calculate numbers relevant to attain this secondary personality that makes up the overall balance for each name you have. Undertone is another set of personalities that are an *undercurrent*, or, represent *underlying* personality traits.

Most people find their primary number is the dominant of the two. My research shows at least 95% of the population is primary. Those who find their undertone numbers are mostly dominant are not special or different in any way. The cause is related to your date time and place of birth. My investigation so far, indicates a link towards the balance of elements in your astrological chart. I will post any new research and developments on my website www.namesdoctor.com

A conclusive test that does identify your dominant character is to highlight everything that applies to you on both your primary and undertone pages. Most people are dominant in primary by 60% to 85%. Even if you are a

50/50% match, you can still be primary. It takes an overall majority of at least 55% in favor of undertone for you to be sure you are not primary.

Very often you will have one or two names that are *extremely* dominant in undertone, with the primary names scoring relatively low by comparison. This is usually a good indication that you are undertone dominant.

If a personality page has 20 definitions (exclude lowest form and health) and you highlighted 15 definitions, then you are 75% dominant for that page. Do the same for all your pages to find your average score.

The other option, if you are not certain, is calculate both your primary and your undertone chart. Look for prominent events in a specific year. One chart will usually reveal events that you can recognize and relate to within specific years of your life.

If you are undertone, both your primary numbers chart and your events chart, will flip numerically upside down. You will understand this more when you read Chapter Eight, preparing your events chart.

Chapter Five

DON'T SHOOT ME, I'M JUST THE MESSENGER

You are about to read sensitive information for the 64 different personalities and descriptions of the effects created by letters of the alphabet from A to Z. Many of these descriptions read positive. However, some of these descriptions can read very negative.

Unfortunately we live in a bizarre world that can be called heaven and hell. There is so much good to enjoy and yet so much bad to suffer. I was considering leaving out some of the extremely negative descriptions or putting them in a separate chapter at the end of the book. Yes our world is full of thieves, rapists and murderers. Yet our world is also full of brilliant, kind, gentle and considerate people who strive to help others. Sometimes there is a fine line that divides the two. Understanding that line is important.

I must stress most emphatically that you fully understand that the negative and most especially the lowest form definitions with strong remarks like death, violence, murder, cunning, evil, obsessive and life threatening accidents, will not simply happen because somebody's name totals to that number. *It takes a highly irregular combination of personalities/numbers and/or an imbalance of letters from the events chart for the lowest form to show and have any effect.*

Later in this book, I explain what provokes the lowest form, together with examples of real people doing bad things. This incredible system shows you why some people are naturally good, honest and happy. This system also shows you why some people are bad, dishonest, violent or unhappy. This system will show you why some people flip from one to the other. Sometimes, the events chart will pinpoint which years they are most likely to cross the line. You can discover this and more, by understanding a person's name and letter combinations.

Just because somebody owns a fast car does not mean they are going to drive like crazy, have an accident and kill somebody. However, if the same person drinks alcohol and drives like a maniac, to show off in front of friends, the worst can happen.

So please, for now, look on the bright side and ignore the lowest form comments.

Negative definitions do not show or affect a person to any serious degree if they have balanced names. People with balanced names/numbers and balanced letters from each of their names are usually happy. Quite simply, happy people rarely do bad things. Unhappy people in a negative environment are more likely to take drastic measures.

Health; you will see every personality from 1 to 64 has a health advisory. This is an *advisory* to let you know the weakest area relevant to that number. Only when you see the same advisory repeat in two or especially three of your primary names should you take notice, seek reliable professional advice and change your lifestyle as necessary to help compensate. Personality number 8 warns of risk towards growths, tumors and cancer.

I must stress this is just an advisory to indicate you have a slightly higher chance of these problems compared to somebody who does not have an 8.

Like the health warning on a packet of cigarettes, you are at a higher risk if you smoke. Do all smokers get lung cancer—No!

I have many friends of all ages who have no issues despite having one 8 as a primary number. I have a friend with one primary 8 and a big mole (growth) on her cheek. Another friend with two 8's had to remove a malignant spot on his arm. However, he has spent most of his life on the beach in Florida. Keith Richards of The Rolling Stones has two 8's, yet despite many years of smoking and excessive chemical drug abuse, he has had no problems in this area made known to the public. You can never be too careful. If you do have an 8 in your primary numbers, or especially two or three, then I suggest you take more notice and act accordingly. Live a healthy lifestyle and get regular professional advice. The number 8 in your undertone numbers will have less or little effect compared to a primary number.

You will see reference to **introvert** and **extrovert. Introvert** does not have to mean this person is a recluse. Usually it indicates a reserved sensible character. Likewise, **extrovert** does not always mean totally outrageous. Obviously if you have two introvert or two extrovert names, the tendency is going to increase. If you have one of each then you are likely to switch from one to another, sometimes with little or no warning. This may be confusing to your friends but is not usually harmful unless other names with excess nerves add to the mix.

The terms **mental nerves** and **physical nerves** pop up frequently. Do not be alarmed. This does not necessarily indicate hysteria or a nervous breakdown. One name with nerves can often be very good. Albert Einstein, Steve Jobs, Bill Gates, Richard Branson and many other brilliant people have two names with nerves. Balance is the key.

Please continue with the book, read your name and become more familiar with the way this process works. If you find a lot of **negatives** and some **lowest** form definitions show in your names, the chapters later in this book will explain why.

Chapter Six

HOW TO READ YOUR NAME

This is where the fun starts. If you follow these step-by-step instructions you will find it easy and rewarding. I suggest you start with your own name first and then move on to somebody you know well like a family member or good friend. It can be fun calculating and reading the names of celebrities and high profile people. It requires a little practice to get it right, but as long as you gather all their names including their mother's maiden name and date of birth, you can see the *Reality.*

When calculating your name, you may do well to share the information with somebody you feel comfortable enough to confide with. Most of us tend to deny some aspects in our own lives. Your friend will correct you here and there with little details you may overlook. Doing this with your partner can be quite an adventure as you see each of your names reveal more and more about you to each other.

I assume you have already calculated all your numbers using the method described in the previous chapter. If you have not peeked at the definitions for your names in Chapter Seven, give yourself a pat on the back.

First, read your individual personality pages, both primary and undertone for your first name, then your other names one by one in order. When you read the numbers for your family name, you will of course see definitions that also apply to your parents and siblings. Some definitions will apply to them but not to you. This is because one name can balance, modify or alter the outcome of another. Other family members will not have the same combination of numbers as you. Even if you carry the same exact names as your mother or father, they will have a different mother's maiden name and mostly likely be born on a different day.

You should find a high percentage of the definitions on your primary personality pages relate you. Remember it is likely your undertone numbers will show a lot less information relevant to you. Do not be alarmed if each primary name definition is not 100% you. This is because you are made up from the combination of several names. The positive or negative from one name will balance, tone down, alter or modify another.

Also remember, we progress as we grow older. Early in life we can be young and reckless. Older in life we can become more considerate or less tolerant. During the span of your life, you will fulfill many of the definitions in all of your names.

YOU ARE THE COMBINATION OF ALL YOUR NAMES

Photocopy the pages in chapter seven relevant to your numbers. Yes, this information is copyrighted, but I give you full permission to do this for your personal use. If this is for professional purposes, you will do better to spend just a few $ dollars and download all of my work documents and calculation programs from my website www.namesdoctor.com

Take a green pen and highlight all the good definitions you recognize about yourself. Then take a red pen and highlight all the negative definitions you recognize about yourself. It is very important you be honest, do not over or under estimate yourself. Also consider the way other people see you. As I mentioned previously, I highly recommend you share this information with someone close to you for a second opinion. There can be points you do not see that your friend will notice. If there is something you recognize about yourself from the past that was you, even if it no longer is you, simply underline it for reference. If a word or two within a sentence is not you, but the rest of the sentence is, mark everything except those words.

Take a pencil and circle any definitions that repeat in each of the pages. Write 2 or 3 at the side so that you know how often this definition repeats. If a definition repeats, it confirms the validity. If it repeats more than once, you might want to write *very* next to it.

Now go back and read only the highlighted definitions from all your personality pages. You are the natural blend of all these features.

You may find it beneficial to lay the pages across a table so you can visually scan, read and understand who you really are and why you live your life the way you do.

HOW CAN YOU BENEFIT FROM THIS INFORMATION

First, we tend to make decisions no matter how big or small, based on our emotions. Usually, this is wrong. Decisions should be made based upon logic unless you are naturally intuitive. Later we realize we made bad choices and have to undo the problems or worse we have to suffer the consequences. Next time you make a decision, stop and think about whom you really are and the way you react to situations based upon your name personalities. Then start using logic or combine your intuitive gift to make the right choice, the first time.

Second, now that you know your strong points, take advantage of them with pride. If a definition says you have talent for a specific area within your career, go for it, with confidence. Now that you know your weak points, keep them small and under your control. If a definition says you can be too impulsive or too argumentative, when a situation arises, stop, think and take control.

Third, if you have one name creating problems, consider removing that name entirely. You can replace it with a positive initial, or simply change the way it is spelled. This must be done with great care and skill or you can end up in more trouble than you started with. However, a new replacement name, especially if complimented with positive letters, can bring out the best in *all* your names.

Fourth, if health issues repeat, the more times they repeat the more you should pay attention as this can be a potential weak spot.

Chapter Seven

PERSONALITIES 1 to 64

This chapter has 64 pages. Each page defines one of the 64 different personalities. Use this information to learn who you really are and then move on to discover the influencing forces created by the letters in your names affecting your daily life.

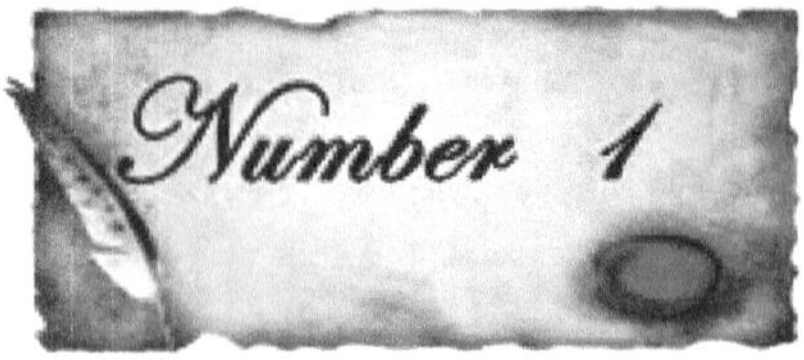

Quick and alert but can produce too much energy.

Can be extrovert.

This definition is *greatly* influenced by your other names/letters/events.

This number cannot form a name but can be used as an initial. Letters A, J and S all represent 1. Your birthday can represent 1 and this is where it is most commonly used in. This can be a good number, extremely powerful, sometimes too powerful in its pure form as 1. Numbers that reduce to 1 have varying levels of high activity. Some need less than average sleep.

You can be very quick and alert, mentally, physically or both. You have a good sense of humor. You are intelligent, creative and inventive in your ways of thinking. You have a love for science and/or the arts. You have such tremendous energy you very often cannot keep still. This number can affect you mentally or physically in many ways, some for better or some worse.

Positive: You are capable of interpreting and executing difficult tasks. You have a strong power of concentration and you are very exact to detail. You can become deeply absorbed in your own thoughts.

Career: You can progress and advance where ever you focus. You are a natural leader, an inventor, engineer or pioneer. This name offers many career possibilities.

Love: Relationships can suffer unless your partner is very understanding.

Negatives: Your career and interests can dominate your life leading to neglect of both yourself and others. You can become selfish and critical. You are easily irritated if interrupted during moments of deep thought.

Lowest Form: You can be too sharp, cunning evil and obsessive.

Health: Take care of your lungs and breathing apparatus. Avoid pollution and smoking.

Very good potential. Very active Brain.

Quiet and Intelligent.

This definition is balanced or altered by influences from your other names.

You are quiet, gentle and sincere. You need harmony, hate trouble and should avoid quarrels. You can be romantic and dreamy. You may appear introvert to others by your quiet demeanor, but you will strongly protect or stand and fight battles for others. You have high standards. Home, family and partner are very important to you.

Positive: You are well mannered, knowledgeable, with an interest in science. You have power to complete great things with little or no action.

Career: Good mind, good eye for numbers, you learn fast so open to many professions including accountancy. You are at your best in a quiet environment.

Love: Passion for the opposite sex but can fall in love too quickly.

Negative: Take care not to overwork the brain. You can focus too much.

Lowest Form: You become ignorant and conceited. You lack skill and knowledge. The opposite of what is normally associated to this number.

Health: To overwork the brain will cause eyestrain and headaches.

Double digit numbers that reduce to 2 and birthdays can represent this number. This is where the number 2 is used most for Name Reality.

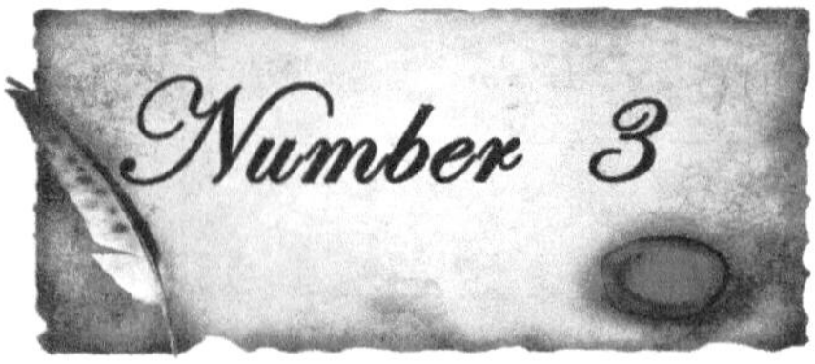

Energetic. Very caring. Ability to take control.

This definition is balanced or altered by influences from your other names.

You are very energetic, giving and helpful. You show good initiative. You will take control of a situation or defend and take care of anyone who needs help. You are fond of children and animals. This number likes or can show talent for music, singing or acting. Birthdays can represent this number and this is where it is most commonly used in Name Reality.

Positive: You are obliging. You will keep promises. You are lively and fun to be with. When positive, people like to be in your company.

Career: Your caring nature will make you good within any caring profession. This can include anything from a vet or physician to somebody who also protects people, like working for the military or police force.

Love: You are normally very kind and loving but take care not to be controlling and spoil a good relationship.

Negative: You can be a dreamer and tend to exaggerate sometimes. Over doing things or wasting time leaves you drained low and often irritable. Take care not to be over caring and too controlling because this will drive away the people who normally love to be in your company.

Lowest Form: Lack of concentration and lack of action when most needed yet you still expect full control of whatever may be going on.

Health: Take care of the Throat.

Double digit numbers that reduce to 3 and birthdays can represent this number. This is where the number 3 is used most for Name Reality.

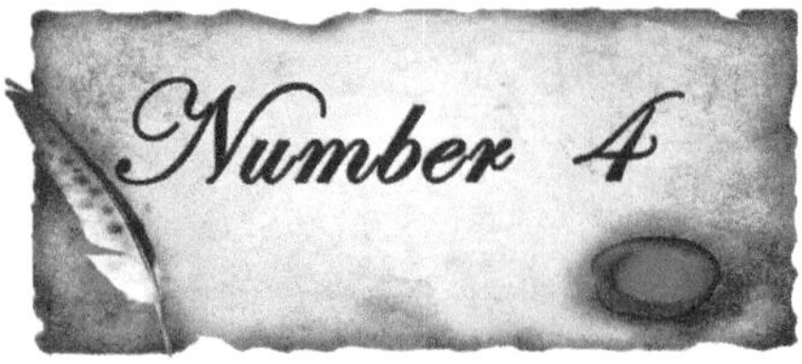

Pendulum, you can be very good, bad or both. Extrovert. Guard temper.

This definition is *greatly* influenced by your other names/letters/events.

Your personality can swing good or bad depending mostly upon balance from your other names and sometimes from negative letters or events. When balanced, life is good. You can attain high levels for yourself and help those around you. When other names add a negative balance, your life can take a bad direction and you can sink to the lowest levels. You love to travel, especially by water and overseas. You are more fortunate and will find more friends in the SW of City, County or Country. Living in the NE can make you unhappy. You are normally cautious with money, you like to save and invest, but can flip the other way and spend to impress. You have good common sense but when negative, your opposing nature can lead to foolish acts. 4 is the opposite of 9.

Positives: You are industrious. Good with your hands. Good teaching others.

Career: You will work hard but only if you enjoy it. Those with negative balance will prefer to socialize.

Love: You like being made a fuss of and the center of attention.

Negatives: You can have a temper, be violent foolish impulsive jealous and possessive which affects relationships and health. You can be controlling and too opposing. Two extrovert names can make you dictatorial and dominating. 4 is the opposite of 9. The two do not mix well especially if combined with one or especially two names with mental or physical nerves.

Lowest Form: You can be hateful, cruel, evil and egotistic. Your temper can become serious and lead to fatal consequences.

Highest form: Expect development of yourself and ability to teach others.

Health: Take extra care of the heart and blood circulation.

Double digit numbers that reduce to 4 and birthdays can represent this number. This is where the number 4 is used most for Name Reality.

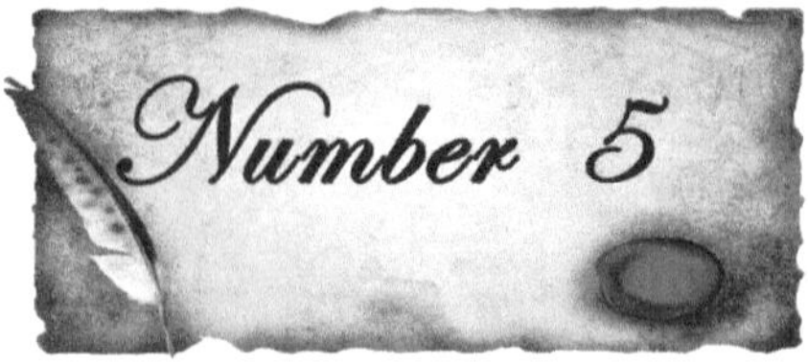

Fast paced. Clever. Very energetic.

Excess physical nerves.

This definition is *greatly* influenced by your other names/letters/ events. Too many names with physical or mental nerves can put this person into overload requiring careful examination.

You are very energetic mentally and physically. You have a good versatile mind with a wide range of interests and foresight. You are good communicating with others but only if they can keep up with your fast pace. Your interests spread far and wide from writing reading languages literature science and philosophy to psychic subjects.

Positives: You are charitable, logical and optimistic. You recognize rule and order and will adhere to this as long as your names have balance.

Career: Your attention to detail enables you to succeed anywhere you focus, in law, commerce, science, literature, teaching, or the arts.

Love: You love kindness and simple honest pleasures.

Negatives: You can fail to achieve and procrastinate from overactive mind. You can be too energetic and talk too much. Too many E's in your names will likely make you impulsive. You can be too kind and too generous, depleting yourself.

Lowest Form: You can show weakness of character and be easily misled. Your respect for law and order turns to disrespect. Evil associations or actions can damage the body and spirit.

Health: Liver/gall bladder is sensitive. Take extra care. Avoid excess alcohol, fatty foods and pollution. Nerves and stress create problems.

Double digit numbers that reduce to 5 and birthdays can represent this number. This is where the number 5 is used most for Name Reality.

Number 6

Peace and tranquility.

Creative, this name often produces artistic talent.

This definition is balanced or altered by influences from your other names.

You are ambitious, you can be very successful. When happy you progress rapidly. You need and appreciate peace and quiet. You dislike sudden noise or being in a loud environment. Though sometimes have to put up with it. This will drain upon you until you find calmness elsewhere. Relationships and home are very important. You will conceal fears and worries, waiting to fix problems later when the time is more appropriate.

Positives: You have a love or desire for beauty and harmony which often shows in your appearance and belongings.

Career: Your creativity gives many career prospects, often within the arts. Love of the land can lead to geology, farming, gardening and landscaping.

Love: Can be successful in love. Harmony with your partner is important.

Negatives: You can be too materialistic. Life becomes a battle if people oppose your plans and dreams. Concealment, especially if F is first letter of your name, either you concealing or people concealing things from you.

Lowest Form: Your creativity diminishes meaning thoughtless plans will usually fail. You will steal to gain money and power. You crave material possessions.

Health: Take care of the Heart and Hearing, avoid all stress and strain.

Double digit numbers that reduce to 6 and birthdays can represent this number. This is where the number 6 is used most for Name Reality.

You have great potential.

Intuitive, good with business and communications.

This definition is balanced or altered by influences from your other names.

You have an excellent mind, executive ability and communication skills. You are friendly, fun to be with, talkative, outward going but emotionally reserved and reluctant to reveal feelings. You appreciate nature.

Positive: You are organized, determined, patient and always complete difficult tasks. Expect long life with all faculties. You can be giving and concerned for others.

Career: Your ability to get noticed for your business talent brings you success in almost any area you desire. You are capable handling big projects, organizing and working with large crowds of people.

Love: You do not show your emotions unless balanced by other names.

Negative: You can be too set in your ways and inflexible.

Lowest Form: You will face danger of deceit and restriction by others especially in business.

Health: You will generally enjoy good health. Your spleen is a very important life force. Avoid removing it unless extremely necessary.

When the number 7 is used as the initial G or Y it helps bring out the positive in all your other names and releases your full potential enabling you to achieve your goals. Of course the overall balance of all your names is still very important. Initials G or Y are not a magic formula or a quick fix.

Double digit numbers that reduce to 7 and birthdays can represent this number. This is where the number 7 is used most for Name Reality.

Number 8

Always striving. Appreciate calm.

Travel. Guard health.

This definition is balanced or altered by influences from your other names.

You are always striving to get ahead so, many with this name are often slim. You are usually good and particular when it comes to choosing business associates, friends and where you live. You love nature and the outdoor life. You need peace and quiet to relax. You like the countryside even if you live in the city. You do like to talk, sometimes too much.

Positive: You are active and have a lot of energy. Good with words both spoken and written. You are sincere and loyal. You believe in fairness and usually make good decisions. Travel comes with this name, enjoy it!

Career: You work well with honorable people. You are good working in the city or with large crowds. You are very creative and should use this ability within your work. You are attracted to outdoors. This can show in your choice of occupation, but more often as recreation, because for you this becomes a form of relaxation. Football on Saturday and fishing on Sunday as a good example.

Love: You sometimes choose virtuous associations. Good for business but this means you can sometimes miss out on true love.

Negative: This name can bring stress strain and make life difficult, especially if the letter H is in your name, but you usually handle it well. Beware as bad or jealous friends may stab you in the back.

Lowest Form: Destruction, hostility and struggle leads to confrontations.

Health: Stress and strain will affect the stomach. *You are at more risk for tumors growths and cancer with this number. Stress and any form of pollution should be avoided. Live a healthy lifestyle to compensate and seek regular professional advice as a precaution.*

Double digit numbers that reduce to 8 and birthdays can represent this number. This is where the number 8 is used most for Name Reality.

Introvert. When focused, you excel,

when not, you dream and deliberate.

This definition is balanced or altered by influences from your other names.

You are strong and flexible, yet quiet and sometimes serious. You like music, especially dreamy or sad compositions. You are intelligent. You notice small details that other people often miss. 9 is the opposite of 4.

Positive: You are creative with a strong imagination. You have deep insight and you can be intuitive even psychic. You are sympathetic when necessary. You will forgive but never forget.

Career: You would make good writer or author.

Love: You do love your home and home life. Some with a 9 come from a broken home. There is a tendency to separation and divorce in your life, but you are sensitive and compassionate.

Negative: You tend to underestimate yourself and you will exaggerate the importance of friends. Relationships can be stressful. You can brood over problems, worry needlessly and sometimes become depressed. You prefer being in the background, but given a push you can get ahead. 9 is the opposite of 4. The two do not mix well especially if combined with one or especially two other names with nerves.

Lowest Form: You can be hypocritical, fraudulent, cunning and deceitful.

Health: Physical stress can upset the stomach and digestion. Groin area can be weak. You can be prone to sexually transmitted diseases.

Double digit numbers that reduce to 9 and birthdays can represent this number. This is where the number 9 is used most for Name Reality.

Number 10

(R1)

You are very energetic, quick and active

This definition is balanced or altered by influences from your other names.

You are independent and a natural leader at home or work. You have the ability to rise from a low to a high position. You have clear mental vision. You are normally bright cheerful happy optimistic and get on well with people. Very active in work and some with this number will enjoy active sports. You like things in their place, especially at work.

Positive: You are constructive, inventive, organized, determined and witty. You have a strong power of concentration. You are very passionate about what you do.

Career: Excellent executive ability. Good with figures plans and drawings.

Love: You will work hard to provide for yourself and those you love.

Negative: You can focus too much on your life and forget others. You can be anal wanting things too much in order or in the correct place.

Lowest Form: You can experience career loss from important positions.

Health: Generally good health, but guard lungs and breathing apparatus.

Number 11

(R11)

Pendulum, very good, bad or both.

Excess mental nerves.

This definition is *greatly* influenced by your other names/letters/ events. Too many names with physical or mental nerves can put this person into overload requiring careful examination.

You can be independent helpful very giving and generous, or demand love and attention. You have a very active mind, great vitality with tremendous energy or outbursts sometimes at the expense of dangerous nervous strain. You prefer city to country life. Thus like to be around people. You can be extravagant.

Positive: When positive you can be lenient and caring for those less fortunate. You are fond of learning and very often talented. You have strength in character but can be rash and reckless.

Career: You can be successful in travel or worldwide business.

Love: You need a very mature minded extremely understanding partner.

Negative: When negative you can be bluntly outspoken and easily led astray. You can have emotional outbursts, be irritable and bad tempered through too much nervous energy.

Lowest Form: Wasteful, extravagant, arrogant and abuse your power.

Highest form: Your desire for knowledge can lead to great achievement and recognition. It takes balance in all your names to attain this level.

Health: Nervous energy affects blood pressure, headaches and digestion, yet you have power to endure. Study and mentally active exercise will help burn up your excess energy providing relief.

Number 12

(R3)

Very nice personality

but take care not to be too giving and caring.

This definition is balanced or altered by influences from your other names.

You are kind and loving and giving by nature. You are affectionate to children animals and people. You are courteous and appreciate good manners. You can be talkative and expressive. Travel comes with this name. You like mystery, have a tendency to daydream and you like to eat frequently. Some with this name show talent for music and acting. You should not be over ambitious in both your life and career.

Positive: Your excellent intuition with foresight can show psychic ability. Discretion is one of your virtues, or vices if you are hiding something.

Career: You are usually called upon for a giving or caring profession, but be careful it does not dominate your life and wear you down both mentally and physically.

Love: You are caring loving giving and romantic, but you need and appreciate equal love in return.

Negative: Giving too much to others can be very draining. Self discipline is very important for this name to flourish and prosper. Set realistic goals.

Lowest Form: Selfish. Strong sexual desires.

Health: Avoid becoming drained. Take care of your throat.

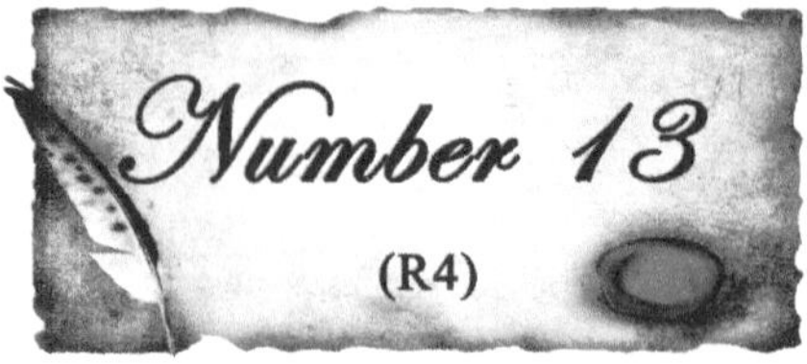

Extrovert. This name represents constant change.

Guard temper.

This definition is *greatly* influenced by your other names/letters/events.

You are very sociable and usually affectionate by nature. Love travel, especially by water. This name represents constant change bringing many life experiences. You do not like to be alone, all relationships are very important to you. You can be sensitive. You are easily hurt by obtuse remarks. You appear confident and extrovert, but tend to worry about small or minor details. The owner of this name need not worry about the superstition created by the number 13.

Positive: You are practical and usually good with your hands, especially in mechanical lines.

Career: You are a quick learner and adaptable. This makes you good with people. You can be good at teaching. Be it professional or mentoring.

Love: You can be faithful and sociable with an affectionate nature. You appreciate the opposite sex and will often show it in your mannerism.

Negative: Your temper needs control. When negative, jealousy upsets relationships and career. You will discriminate or be class conscious. Greed can be your downfall.

Lowest Form: You will walk away from a problem unnecessarily rather than face up and fix it, bringing disaster. Greed can make you dangerous.

Health: Stress or over excitement affects the Blood Circulation and Heart.

Number 14

(R5)

Extrovert. Physical nervous energy.

Bright. Alert. Usually successful

This definition is *greatly* influenced by your other names/letters/events. Too many names with physical or mental nerves can put this person into overload requiring careful examination.

You are versatile, practical, bright and energetic. Sharp and alert, you notice the smallest of details. You are a fast learner. Love of justice. You have the ability to succeed whenever you put your mind to something.

Positive: You can be successful in anything connected with people. You are good with written and spoken words. You will fight other people's battles if not your own.

Career: When positive this name is open to many career possibilities. You would make excellent teacher writer or lawyer.

Love: The critical side of your nature can delay marriage until later in life.

Negative: You expect too much from work colleagues or friends who simply lack your fast pace. You can be impulsive critical and unpredictable. You can express opinions without full knowledge. Vanity will be your downfall.

Lowest Form: Selfish. Wrong friends lead you astray. You will lie.

Health: Liver/gall bladder and Nerves, This number represents the body itself, so health can be sensitive. However the strongest tendency is towards good health. If there is a problem you have strength for recovery.

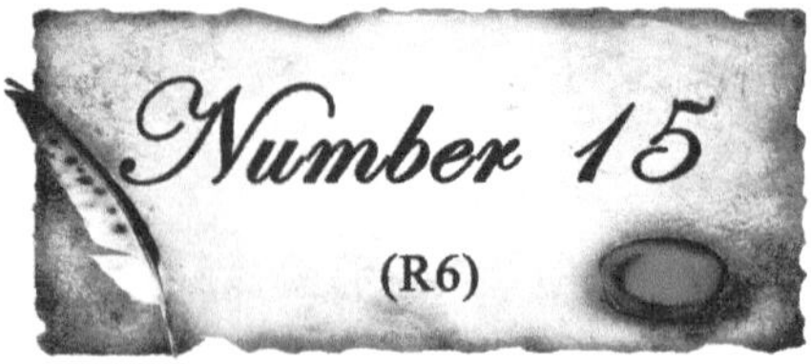

Introvert. Quiet, quick, often with a brilliant mind.

This definition is balanced or altered by influences from your other names.

You need melody and harmony in all areas of your life. You dislike sudden loud or noisy discordant environments. You have a love for music with ability to play an instrument. You prefer to live life quietly and help others but you will speak out whenever it becomes necessary.

Positive: You are determined. You have pureness of thought. You have a versatile vivid imagination. Very quick to learn with a brilliant mind, yet modesty is one of your virtues.

Career: You have artistic and creative ability but you prefer not to be the center of attention. Love science and the arts. You can be successful in religious or spiritual lines.

Love: You do need time for yourself. You are loyal and sincere. Your friends will do well to respect you by not being too demanding. Marriage does not always work for this name.

Negative: Beware dreaming of non-viable schemes. Too many O's in this name make for physical slowness, over caution or slow to make a decision.

Lowest Form: You can be too subtle and crafty for your own good.

Health: Take care of the Heart and Liver.

Number 16

(R7)

This number is abnormal to the usual 7

in that it has excess mental nerves.

Extrovert. Life on the edge.

Stress can provoke mental nerves.

This definition is *greatly* influenced by your other names/letters/events.

You are very ambitious, expressive and determined. This name attracts speculators and high flyers in the business world, but beware as overconfidence and impulsive spending can be your downfall. You should learn to be satisfied with enough. Avoid high places if you do not already do so. You like music. Some have a distinctive or good voice.

Positive: You are brave, loyal friendly and honorable.

Career: You have creative and or artistic ability. You can enjoy anything that stimulates your mind from banking and finance to geology, mining or even chemistry. If you run your own business or have a high position take notice of these definitions and avoid potential problems.

Love: You need a very understanding partner.

Negative: When negative you have a tendency to lose focus through an over active mind. You can fall from a high position, bankruptcy or debts will lead to extreme stress. Avoid gambling. Other names that counter balance with control or good business sense will reduce this flaw.

Lowest Form: Lack of inner peace can lead to mental breakdown. Lack of regular rule will lead to wild movements and evil issues.

Health: When happy with balanced names, you will live a long and healthy life. Stress seriously provokes nerves which can affect the brain.

Number 17

(R8)

Happy and fun loving with a good sense of humor.

Guard health.

This definition is balanced or altered by influences from your other names.

You are bright happy and very intuitive. Good with written and spoken words. Travel comes with this name usually for both work and pleasure. You love the outdoors for calm and relaxation and you like music. This is a good name for business but beware not to be over optimistic.

Positive: This is a safe name for travel, which is good considering the statement above. You have determination to overcome obstacles.

Career: Anything with travel and involving the public. Love for science, chemistry, literature and the arts.

Love: Both sexes like you for your humor and child like fun.

Negative: Can be sulky and bad tempered when under stress.

Lowest Form: Lack of faith or belief leads to uncertainty and procrastination.

Health: Digestion is sensitive.

Number 18

(R9)

Introvert. You have a great heart. Stay focused to stay on top.

This definition is *greatly* influenced by your other names/letters/events.

When happy you shine and thrive. When sad you become introvert. You have great potential and are capable of great things when you stay focused and positive. You have a great love for home and family. Usually quiet. You have a strong imagination and dry sense of humor. The small things in life can bring the most pleasure. Sometimes this name is unlucky or plans just do not work out. To keep on track or get back on track, it is very important you focus.

Positive: When happy, life is good. You may appear reserved, but will stand up for truth, justice and what you believe in with integrity. You usually win disputes.

Career: When positive and focused you have many opportunities. Possibilities include writer, councilor, lawyer or physician to name a few.

Love: Not always lucky in love. You need an understanding partner who gives you time out when you need to be alone. You can be very romantic. Watch the sunset from a tranquil location is your ideal way to end the day.

Negative: With negative influence you can be too dreamy and lose focus. You can be hypocritical when your life is not going well. When sad you can feel very low and want to be in your own space.

Lowest Form: You will fall into a false sense of security. You will likely enter into unprofitable associations, especially with women.

Health: Groin area is weakest. Avoid physical strain and avoid sexually transmitted diseases. Also take care of the Heart.

Number 19

(R1)

**You can be very caring. You love home and family life.
Quick mind.**

This definition is balanced or altered by influences from your other names.

You are friendly, loving, thoughtful, giving and easy to please. Make sure people do not take advantage of your good nature. You are modest and brave when necessary. You have a serious nature but also a good sense of humor. You have a quick mind and are good with constructive words.

Positive: You have an excellent memory. You are inventive and good at fixing problems. This is a very safe name for fire water and high places. You have the ability to focus on spirituality or the understanding of life, people will listen and follow.

Career: You can be successful in anything you put your mind to, especially with land, property and buildings near water or low lying land.

Love: Your love of home and need to improve the home can lead to an early marriage. Friends and partnerships are vital for happiness.

Negative: You can be too loving, caring and easy to please. People will take advantage and walk all over you. Get firm and learn to say no.

Lowest Form: You can feel low or depressed from failure, despair or problems in the home. Strong sexual desires.

Health: Danger to Chest Lungs and Breathing. Avoid all forms of pollution and smoking.

Number 20

(R2)

Good personality, good intentions, eye for detail, but can lack confidence.

This definition is balanced or altered by influences from your other names.

You are quiet, gentle thoughtful and conscientious yet quick and alert. You like peace and harmony and will strongly promote this. You can have psychic and spiritual interests.

Positive: You have an enquiring mind and a good eye for detail. Your intentions are always good, even if the result is not always positive.

Career: Artistic. Good eye for detail. You could be an architect or physician but beware of negative thoughts restricting your progress.

Love: You are thoughtful kind and gentle towards loved ones and animals. Unfortunately you can be rendered unhappy by contention in the home. Yet this name when female, make excellent mothers.

Negative: Negative influences make you self-critical and blame yourself. Stress and strain, problems past and present with negative thoughts about the future can become overwhelming.

Lowest Form: Weakness in character can lead to bad choices, drug or alcohol abuse, wasting time or simply being cruel.

Health: Headaches, brain or head problems. You can be prone to food poisoning.

Number 21

(R3)

Naturally caring, bright and

brilliant with excellent potential.

This definition is balanced or altered by influences from your other names.

You are extremely alert, bright brilliant and intelligent. You are naturally caring and protecting. You have a love for music, often with the ability to sing or act. You can be fond of nature, gardens plants or the perfumes they emit. You may have an interest in herbal remedies. This name will often retain youthful qualities.

Positive: You are careful with details. You like to study if a subject lures your attention. Some with this name like astronomy. Any form of literature, books, writing, reading and all aspects of the arts will appeal to most with this name. You are quick to learn and you can be successful.

Career: Anything mentally stimulating. This is a good name for anything linked to the world of entertainment.

Love: You need a demonstrative partner to match your caring nature.

Negative: You are quick to retaliate verbally if criticized. You can be impulsive when under stress. You will let opportunities slip by if the letter U is in your names.

Lowest Form: Ignorant, prejudice, impulsive, liable to make errors.

Health: Take care of the Throat.

Number 22

(R22)

Capable of great achievement or great disaster. Extrovert. Excess mental nervous energy. Brilliant ability can swing Good, Bad or Both, influenced by other names. Does not reduce to 4 but can show similarity to both 4 and 11 including lowest and highest forms.

This definition is *greatly* influenced by your other names/letters/ events. Too many names with physical or mental nerves can put this person into overload requiring careful examination.

This name has a strong impulse to wander (in a good or bad direction). This can be physically or just mentally wandering in your mind. You love travel, especially abroad. This name is generally fortunate when positive. Usually good making money when positive, but can be too extravagant when negative. You love social life, but sometimes too much when negative. You need to balance career and social life or combine both. This is a safe name for travel.

Positive: When positive you can have a beautiful character. You can be creative, artistic, a philanthropist. You are kind, helpful and generous.

Career: Travel entertainment commerce shipping teacher counselor healer. When positive this name has many career prospects.

Love: Tendency for separation and divorce

Negative: Greed will be your downfall if not controlled. If life is not going well or other names lack balance you can be easily led astray, unable say no, show weak character and people will not take you seriously.

Lowest Form: Extravagant, weak character can drop to the lowest levels.

Highest form: Development of self and others. Desire for knowledge can lead to great achievement and recognition.

Health: Be careful of nerves and nerves affecting the brain.

Number 23

(R5)

Physical nerves. Active. Intelligent,

but can face many difficulties. Stress.

This definition is *greatly* influenced by your other names/letters/ events. Too many names with physical or mental nerves can put this person into overload requiring careful examination.

Physical nerves can make you active and intelligent, but life is not always easy. You can face many obstacles and difficulties throughout the years. You have a versatile mind. You are intelligent and quick to learn. You may have an interest in gardens, perfume and plants and perhaps herbs or alternative medicine. You enjoy country life even if your work keeps you in the city. You like your independence.

Positive: You believe strongly in law order and honor. You are good with languages, even if it is being well versed in your native tongue. You often gain favor with those in position of authority. This can be very much to your advantage if you use this good fortune wisely.

Career: Any form of communications, literature/designer/architect. Some people with this number have a gift or interest in astronomy. You will work hard for security but take care not to slack or people will take advantage when you least expect it.

Love: Compatibility is essential for a lasting relationship with this name.

Negative: When negative this name is prone to oppression, difficult or unfortunate situations. Stress increases worry, uncertainty and problems. These problems are very often within the home. Separation will likely follow. When negative you will give but expect something in return.

Lowest Form: Beware, your greed for money will become a problem. You can be very jealous, resistant, audacious and opposing.

Health: Liver/gall bladder is your most sensitive organ. Avoid fatty foods. Stress and strain can trigger nerves and lead some people with this name to alcohol smoking or drugs which will damage your sensitive liver.

Number 24

(R6)

Not one to worry, usually fortunate.

Like peace and quiet.

This definition is balanced or altered by influences from your other names.

You are generally fortunate in worldly affairs and will meet influential people. You like peace quiet harmony and dislike loud discordant noises. You like music. Your artistic side can lead you in this direction if you chose to do so.

Positive: You are truthful and sincere. *Not one to worry*, a good asset to have if your other names indicate stress or nerves. This name will often have a strong voice.

Career: Contacts will advance your work prospects, often through influential women.

Love: There can be quarrels and separation because of career or negative circumstances. You need an understanding partner.

Negative: You can be at risk to a physical fall hurting your lower back or legs, especially from high places or demanding sports. Avoid if you do not already instinctively do so. You can think too highly of yourself and show signs of becoming selfish. You do not always stand firm.

Lowest Form: Arguments lead to separation, exile, fugitive or prison. You can be disruptive, even dangerous and halt progress for no good reason. You natural creativity turns to creating havoc in the lowest form.

Health: Heart, circulation, lower back and legs.

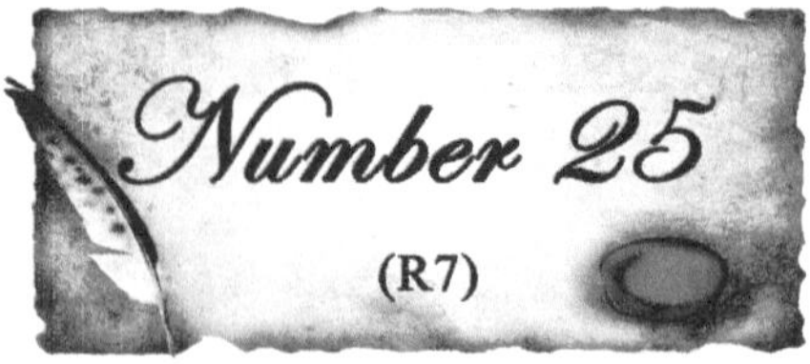

This name is very intuitive.

Good communicating and networking.

This definition is balanced or altered by influences from your other names.

You are very intuitive and have potential psychic ability. You love solving mysteries. You like nature and are usually safe on water. You appreciate time alone to relax.

Positive: You are sincere, determined and very often successful. You gain from experience. You will help the less fortunate.

Career: You are a hard worker and very often successful through contacts. Communication skills are one of your virtues.

Love: You are sociable, loving and sharing with family.

Negative: You tend to over prolong projects, career and relationships. You can be stubborn, but usually because you are right.

Lowest Form: Worry, confusion. You can use your psychic ability for harm.

Health: Your spleen is a very important life force. Avoid removing it unless extremely necessary.

Number 26

(R8)

Very capable, good with detail.

Secretive. Guard health.

This definition is balanced or altered by influences from your other names.

You may have repressed circumstances early in life. However, this is offset with self-confidence. You are energetic. You may not be aware you have the ability to take charge or control, but this will prevail, especially in times of emergency. You are very good at keeping secrets, yet love to know anything and everything about everybody else. You are fond of mysteries.

Positive: You are good with your hands, especially working with fine detail. Good with study. You are driven and will work hard to achieve your goals.

Career: A clever speaker, usually calm, good with politics or diplomatic departments. You work well with people and would make a good writer or councilor. You would make an excellent detective or spy.

Love: Can be too secretive making communication with partner or loved ones a problem. You often realize this when it is too late.

Negative: Do not like people knowing too much about you. You can be very secretive. For these reasons you would make an excellent burglar.

Lowest Form: You will use your powers to conspire or plan to overthrow.

Health: Stomach is the most delicate organ.

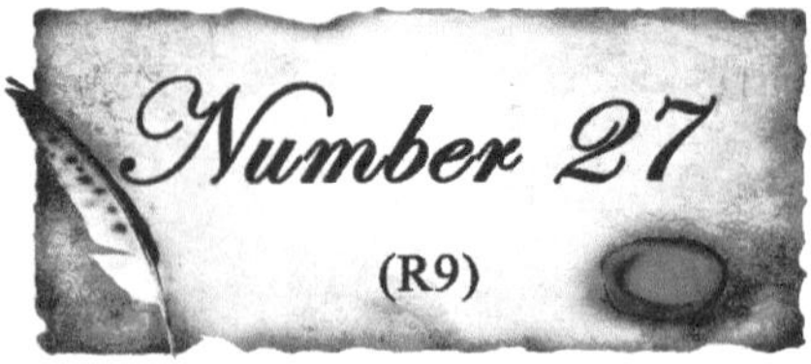

Introvert by number. Organized and

Intuitive but sometimes deliberate.

This definition is balanced or altered by influences from your other names.

You desire to prosper and flourish. You like to study and enjoy sharing your knowledge. Intuitive, trust your first thought. You are good understanding problems and will offer both advice and help to others. You enjoy travel. You are good with your hands. You are usually careful or particular with food and drink. This can lead to an interest in health foods. You will stand for peace and justice. You become more obedient with age.

Positive: Modesty is one of your virtues. You notice small details. You are very organized at home and work. People will take notice and listen to you, do not abuse this gift.

Career: Communications, public speaking, science and the arts. This name produces many distinguished writers. You will enjoy teaching anything to do with nourishing the body or mind.

Love: You are caring and sharing by nature.

Negative: You can be either jealous or in awe of other people's money and possessions, but this will usually make you work harder to achieve more. You can deliberate or worry needlessly over small problems.

Lowest Form: Ignorance and lack of tolerance. Extrovert and excess nerves from other numbers can darken this good name.

Health: Possible digestion problems. Groin area weak, avoid strain.

Number 28

(R1)

Strong personality. Active mind.

You can be very extrovert at times.

This definition is balanced or altered by influences from your other names.

Hard work usually brings you good results and money. You like success and like to be rewarded or taken care of as you do not like to be without. You dislike loud sudden or discordant noises yet you are safe around fire, explosions and heights. You are very direct, preferring simplicity.

Positive: You can show good judgment. You are original and inventive finding solutions. You have a versatile constructive and active mind. You stand firm without fear. If female you have man's strength in a woman's body.

Career: You are a natural leader and very capable in business, often heading or running a company. You are artistic and good with design.

Love: You need to make time in your busy schedule for love.

Negative: Sometimes critical. You can be very extrovert to gain attention. Wrong friends will lead you astray. This name will often like scandal and gossip. You can switch and go any lengths to get ahead.

Lowest Form: Quarrels, arguments. Evil associations will take you down.

Health: Usually good health, but avoid stress and pollution affecting your head and lungs.

Number 29

(R11)

Excess Mental Nerves.

Pendulum, can swing good or bad.

This definition is *greatly* influenced by your other names/letters/ events. Too many names with physical or mental nerves can put this person into overload requiring careful examination.

This name can go two ways. When positive, you are a reformer with desire to change things for the better. Never satisfied with enough, you always have a need for more. You can be suspicious or lack faith in people if you have not had the opportunity to appraise them. When negative, you can be very nervous, mental unrest can make you insecure. You have difficulty making decisions and saying no. You can be generous, but often very extravagant. You are not good around water and heights so it is best you avoid this if you do not already do so. Either way you are very *particular or fussy* about certain things like food and clothes.

Positive: You will work hard to make money. Possessions or a financial stability give you comfort and a sense of security. The glass is half full.

Career: When positive you can be very successful in business to secure your need for money. When negative nothing seems to work well for long.

Love: You distrust most people so you like to be around family and friends.

Negative: The glass is always half empty, never half full. Your life is full of anxiety and doubt. Your insecurity can make you waste time looking in the wrong places for success. You quickly lose motivation. More nervous names can bring fears phobias and immoral actions.

Lowest Form: You will become fanatical and hypocritical

Health: Mental Nerves and Brain. Stress will lower your immune system.

Number 30

(R3)

Relaxed and stress free. Good Brain.

Take control of situations.

This definition is balanced or altered by influences from your other names.

You are friendly, happy, forgiving and caring. You are good with children and animals. You are strong, steady and modest. Your intentions are always good. You are decisive direct and to the point. This name usually has an interest in theatre, music and arts with a desire write act or sing. Your active brain needs stimulation. You can easily become bored with too much simple routine.

Positive: You have patience and hope. You rarely despair even under great stress. You can take control of a situation and have good control of your emotions. These virtues are very powerful overcoming excess nerves from another name. You dislike violence.

Career: You are very focused, like challenge and are good at what you do. You have a good brain, see the big picture and can handle big projects. You would make good physician or any work in the medical/caring field.

Love: Need a partner who equally returns love and affection.

Negative: You tend to exaggerate sometimes. Too much if your names have negative balance. Your ability to take control can go in the wrong direction, take care you do not become too controlling at home and work.

Lowest Form: Infidelity or disloyal.

Health: Take care of the Throat.

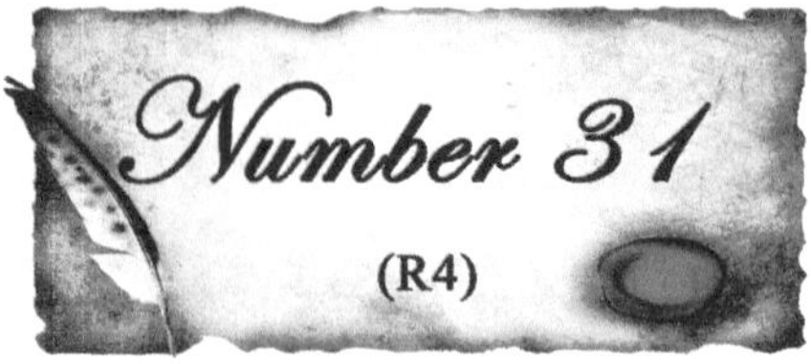

Extrovert by number. Pendulum.

Open Mind or Empty Mind.

This definition is *greatly* influenced by your other names/letters/events.

This number can be quite extrovert. 31 is a pendulum that will swing in a positive or negative direction. Open minded or empty minded depending upon the balance from your other names. You enjoy music, singing or acting. Like astronomy math's sciences and plants or agriculture. You do not like to be alone. Friendships partners and home are very important to you. There are times when you prefer peace and quiet. You like to be in control, this is fine if it is being in control of your life. Take care it is not controlling others.

Positive: When positive you are open minded, versatile and practical. You are caring and will help others.

Career: You are good with legal matters and good working with your hands. Your partner may influence you to work where you have interests or even work together.

Love: As you do not like being alone it is not unusual for this name to marry or settle into a relationship at a young age. However a compatible partner is essential for long term happiness.

Negative: When negative you can have too much emphasis on money and material things. You like peace but will fight with no compunction or restraint. Your temper needs control. You will drain the energy from those around you. Sadly a negative balance from your other names will result in you lacking imagination and be somewhat empty minded.

Lowest Form: An insatiable desire for wealth or gain can lead to extortion.

Health: Excitement or stress will upset blood circulation.

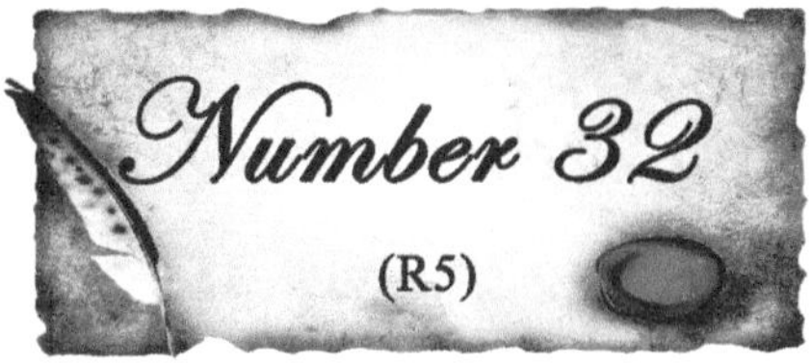

Very active and sociable

with an attractive personality.

This definition is balanced or altered by influences from your other names. Physical nerves are not prominent with this number but can increase with influence from other names.

You are very sociable and popular which brings you into contact with many people from all walks of life. You are good with languages. Those with 32 will have a long life if your other names balance well.

Positive: You are easy going and agreeable yet very strong, determined and enduring. You have perseverance and will find it easy not to rush into making unnecessary changes. You have an excellent memory.

Career: You are very good with lines of communication, both written and spoken. This and your ability to memorize facts can open many doors.

Love: You require a demonstrative partner attentive to your needs and should not rush into relationships for this reason.

Negative: You can become self centered, sarcastic and argumentative.

Lowest Form: Evil associations or actions damage the body and soul.

Health: Take care of the liver/gall bladder.

Number 33

(R6)

Introvert. Work comes with this name.

Good intent. High standards.

This definition is balanced or altered by influences from your other names.

Work is very important, you like financial security and will work hard to provide for yourself and your family. You prepare well for retirement age. You have high standards and do not like to settle for anything less. You have artistic talent so music and acting often come with this name. You can be successful in the city but you do not like crowds and will be happier closer to nature in the country.

Positive: You are usually fortunate financially. You have a lot of energy and you are very organized. You have a strong instinct to protect and care for others, especially the old or less fortunate.

Career: Any caring profession. You can be good with commerce and new enterprises, or follow your love for the arts.

Love: You need a partner who understands your desire to work. You can be undemonstrative and show love by providing.

Negative: Your high standards and desire for financial security can make you work too hard, sometimes neglecting the ones most important to you.

Lowest Form: You will encourage violence or revolts

Health: Heart and throat.

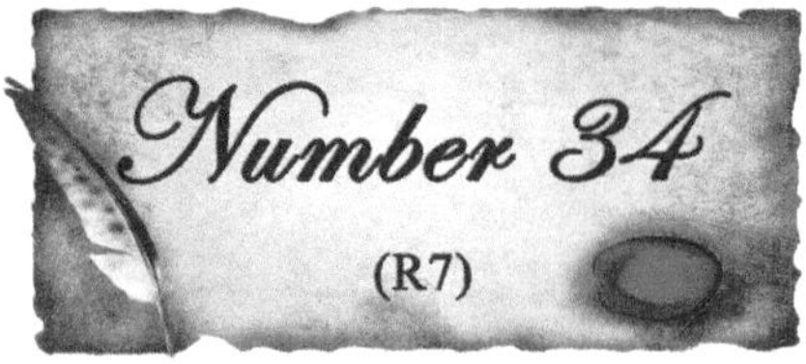

Leadership skills. Capable of great achievements.

This definition is balanced or altered by influences from your other names.

You have leadership skills and executive ability that can show from an early age. You are bright and cheerful. You respond well to problems of your own and those of others. Good temperament. You can be very successful in whatever you chose to do.

Positive: Strong character with will power and determination. You can be very intuitive and show psychic ability. Modesty is one of your virtues.

Career: Any responsible position needing your organizing skills from management to a business owner. You can do well in politics or a position with the military or police.

Love: You need a strong or understanding partner.

Negative: You do not like change. You can be too fixed in ways and dominating. You do not like anger but you will have a temper if provoked.

Lowest Form: Conflicts, quarrels, disloyal.

Health: Stomach sensitive, eat the wrong thing and it will come back up.

Number 35

(R8)

Friendly, active, love tranquility. Guard health.

This definition is balanced or altered by influences from your other names.

You are usually bright friendly and optimistic. You do not like change, in life, home, work or friends. You will travel a lot. You can inherit or gain money from those who remember how you helped them at some time in life. You are calm but can easily become ruffled and distracted, especially when too much is going on. For this reason, relaxation time is important.

Positive: You are trustworthy. Good friends will be friends for life. You will reward those who are loyal. You have integrity. You strive for a peaceful life.

Career: Writer, speaker or anything requiring good attention to detail.

Love: You need a partner who understands your need for stability and dislike of change.

Negative: You can lose focus with stress especially by taking on big or too many projects at the same time.

Lowest Form: Annoying, harassing, cruel and violent.

Health: Potential digestion problems. Be careful what you eat.

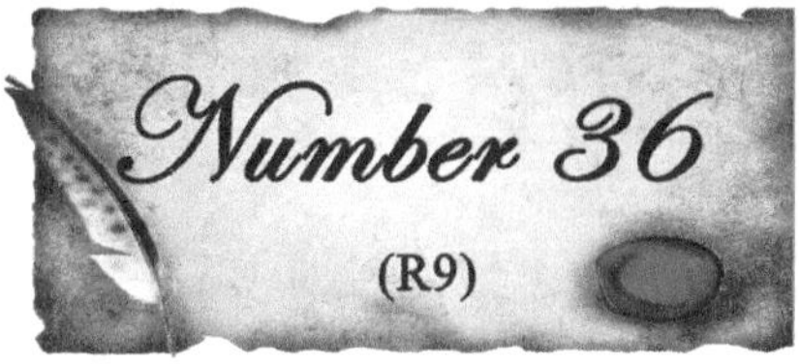

Introvert. Nice personality

but complex and sometimes unlucky.

This definition is *greatly* influenced by your other names/letters/events.

You are quiet, serious and very amiable. You pay attention to detail. You are careful with possessions, particular about your appearance and what you eat. Unfortunately you can go about things the wrong way and often lose what you desire the most. When things go wrong you feel safe at home or with family.

Positive: You are good natured, kind and generous.

Career: You will work hard to attain material things that bring you confidence and joy. You should not be overambitious as failure can follow.

Love: You need a partner who understands your introvert nature.

Negative: You have more than your fair share of losses and disappointments. Depression can bring problems.

Lowest Form: Your deceitful ways means nobody will trust you, especially in business. In turn you become suspicious of everybody.

Health: Your digestion is sensitive and your groin area is weak. Avoid mental stress and physical strain.

Number 37

(R1)

Extrovert. Energetic.

Artistic but some need positive direction.

This definition is *greatly* influenced by your other names/letters/events.

You are quick, energetic with good will and intentions. You like financial security. You have great potential and good business skills but usually need qualified advice and direction to be successful. This can come from another person but best when your names bring balance. You have all the quick traits of personality 10 but lack leadership skills. Read number 10.

Positive: You can be successful through contacts, women in high positions and relations with the opposite sex. You become wise with reflection and experience. You have the potential to inspire the great philosophers, but only when your other names add balance.

Career: Excellent in science, the arts, entertainment and public appearances. You will work hard for material possessions.

Love: You are successful with the opposite sex. However for a happy marriage, you need a partner willing to accept or submit to your ways.

Negative: You can be too domineering, stubborn and usually wrong when you lack direction, as previously mentioned. Bad choices, too much love for money and show or desire to dictate will be your downfall.

Lowest Form: Intermeddling will get you into trouble. Your good intentions are no longer a virtue and flip, meaning you cannot be trusted.

Health: This number must take care of the head and lungs.

Number 38

(R11)

Mental nerves. Bright, intelligent, strong headed but apt to difficulties.

This definition is *greatly* influenced by your other names/letters/ events. Too many names with physical or mental nerves can put this person into overload requiring careful examination.

You are bright, intelligent, generous, and a very good organizer. You have excellent leadership skills. You are somewhat traditional in your ways and may have spiritual or religious beliefs. However sometimes you can be too opinionated. You need positive balance from your other names to achieve both peace and success at the same time.

Positive: You are at your best when busy organizing work or home.

Career: You can be successful financially. You are good with both communications and literary work. Some with this name can be acclaimed or acknowledged for their skills in this area. Management or running a business will suit your abilities.

Love: You can lose respect for a weak partner or quarrel with one who is strong. A well matched partner will bring harmony to your life.

Negative: If the negative side kicks in, difficulties will come your way. You will become quarrelsome and extravagant.

Lowest Form: Hypocritical, cunning, fraudulent.

Health: Nervous energy can lead to brain problems, headaches and insomnia being just two examples.

Number 39

(R3)

Often successful but faced with a lot of problems.

This definition is *greatly* influenced by your other names/letters/events.

Those with this number usually have good health and a potential long life but are often faced with many difficulties. You should live in South West or South West of a street, room or house facing South West. You will not gain any advantage when you live in the North East. Your caring nature can easily flip the opposite way if negative circumstances come into your life.

Positive: If humble you can rise from a low to high position with dignity.

Career: Many with this number can reach high positions, but some will fall.

Love: Strong paternal love for your child, family and very close friends.

Negative: This name faces many difficulties in life. To be a smart ass will be your downfall. When negative you can be cruel and violent.

Lowest Form: Strong sexual desires, or worse, capable of murder, or rape and murder, with no discretion for age or sex.

Health: Throat and heart.

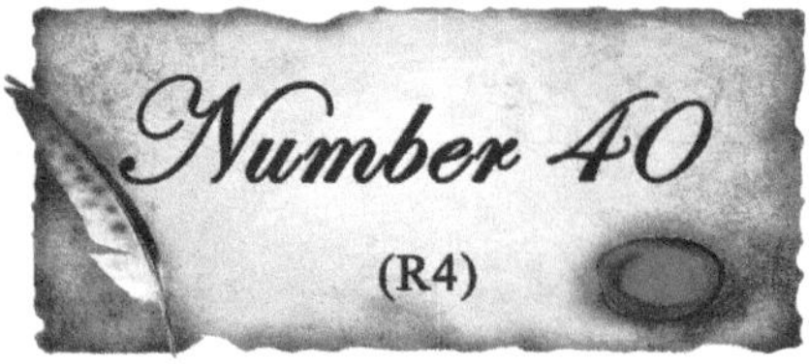

Extrovert. Good with money,

but can have a temper if provoked.

This definition is *greatly* influenced by your other names/letters/events.

You are good with money and like to invest. You love to travel, especially overseas or by water. You have a strong advantage in the South West of a country, county or city. You prefer to forgive and deal gently with problems arising from other people.

Positive: You are honorable, confident and considerate.

Career: You are good with your hands and can succeed with business in literary areas, art, books or printing.

Love: Relationships will be easier if your family friends or partner understand that you sometimes need time and space to be alone.

Negative: There is a tendency to sometimes feel low, but if left alone, you deal with it well. Your temper needs control.

Lowest Form: Opposing, you will seek disputes over differences.

Health: Blood circulation. Avoid stress.

Number 41

(R5)

Excellent control of emotions.

Confident. Smart. Very Active.

This definition is balanced or altered by influences from your other names. Physical nerves are rare in this number but can sometimes show with influence from the undertone or other names.

You are versatile, very energetic physically and mentally. You will likely have religious or spiritual interests. You enjoy study, you like to learn and make improvements. You instinctively know the difference between right and wrong and naturally stay away from danger of any kind. You are good with words, written and spoken.

Positive: You have good control of your emotions, temper or passion. You have the ability to give to others without draining yourself. You are very confident. You can obtain your desires on a grand scale with cultivation and patience.

Career: Political affairs, writing, public speaking or any caring profession.

Love: You love kindness and simple honest pleasures. You need a demonstrative partner who can respond equally with love and affection.

Negative: Some may have trouble keeping up with your fast pace.

Lowest Form: Liable to become a renegade or defector.

Health: Potential trouble with Liver/gall bladder. Avoid pollution and adopt a healthy lifestyle to compensate.

Number 42

(R6)

You try very hard to get ahead

and be a good person.

This definition is *greatly* influenced by your other names/letters/events.

Those who walk in the light have a beautiful soul. The balance from your other names and events throughout your life will greatly influence the outcome of this name in a positive or negative direction. With balance you can be a truly wonderful person always seeking peace and harmony for yourself and others. Negative balance can make life very difficult.

Positive: You have a lot of energy, yet with the ability to remain quiet and calm. You are caring and have artistic / musical talent and may like to sing.

Career: Music or the arts/entertainment. Any caring profession especially those linked to religion or spiritualism.

Love: You have a good heart for marriage.

Negative: With negative influences life can be a struggle, desperately trying to get ahead or to be a good person. Negative balance from other names and negative events can at best create a difficult life or at worst an immoral and destructive or self destructive life.

Lowest Form: Traitor cannot be trusted. Those who choose an immoral life will likely die an early un-natural death.

Health: Take care of the heart, especially when negative.

Number 43

(R7)

Ambition with good intentions.

Frequent travel comes with this name.

This definition is balanced or altered by influences from your other names.

You like an organized life. You are not overly generous but you will help the less fortunate. You do not like being alone. Friends are very important to you. Travel change and movement comes with this name, sometimes by choice, though often by circumstances. You do not like too much routine in your life and will move on rather than put up with boring repetition.

Positive: You are capable of handling multiple projects. You know how to overcome obstacles with words, not force. Positive balance from your other names bring out the excellence in this number, negative balance will taint your performance.

Career: You will work hard to win recognition more than financial reward. You can excel in military life or a corporate type careers where there are good promotion prospects.

Love: You need love in your life. You like attention and can be caring in return.

Negative: When life's not going well you must move on or discontent will follow. You have to work harder than most to reach your goals. You can be at risk of losing position. There is danger from guns or explosions in times of conflict.

Lowest Form: Change of opinion brings quarrel and conflict and you can lack character.

Health: Stomach sensitive, eat the wrong thing and it will come back up.

Number 44

(R8)

Organized and brave.

You desire fame, fortune and recognition.

This definition is balanced or altered by influences from your other names.

You like an organized life. You enjoy using your organizing skills and ability for both work and pleasure. You are very brave. You can excel in military life or in times of emergency. Many with this name win distinction for valor. You will travel for pleasure but more so for business.

Positive: You excel in difficult times when the odds are against you.

Career: You can be successful organizing business and enterprise, often overseas.

Love: You need a partner who understands your need to be in charge.

Negative: If not kept in check, vanity and arrogance will be your downfall.

Lowest Form: Vain selfish and domineering.

Health: Blood circulation and stomach.

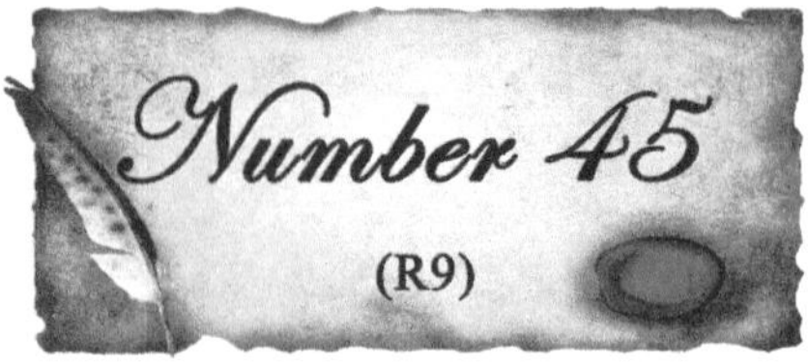

Introvert by number. Thoughtful and caring.

Organized and Prepared.

This definition is balanced or altered by influences from your other names.

You are very thoughtful and caring. You will always put yourself forward to help the elderly or those less fortunate. You like vegetation, flowers, gardening or landscaping. You strongly dislike wicked or arrogant people.

Positive: You are very organized and prepared for any emergency. You learn quickly.

Career: You can be good leading or instructing large numbers of people. Teaching management or running a business will suit your skills.

Love: Your caring nature often leads to an early marriage or a serious steady relationship.

Negative: Sometimes you are too giving. People will take advantage of your caring nature. When necessary you need to stand firm and say no.

Lowest Form: Liable to sudden change or will not finish what you started.

Health: Stomach.

Number 46

(R1)

Intuitive. Strength of mind. Active.

This definition is balanced or altered by influences from your other names.

You have strong intuition or psychic ability. You will advance steadily throughout life. You have very high ideals and sincerely believe in the projects you undertake. You can be successful with those in a position of power. You are good at making money. You will donate to good causes but you can lose money if your projects are too adventurous. You can discover secrets of nature. You truly believe in yourself and what you do. You should live in the south of a country, county or city.

Positive: You are flexible. You have self obedience and strength of mind. You are courageous yet can be discreet.

Career: With your good attributes, knowledge and ability to work hard, you can be good at whatever you chose.

Love: Intuitively know who to love and who to distrust.

Negative: You can be over ambitious. Unfortunately your life can be an emotional roller coaster.

Lowest Form: Unhappy or bored, leading to discontent in all areas of life.

Health: Take care of the lungs.

Number 47

(R11)

Mental Nerves. Sharp. Friendly. Success in Business.

This definition is *greatly* influenced by your other names/letters/ events. Too many names with physical or mental nerves can put this person into overload requiring careful examination.

This name is usually successful. You are friendly and have a love of justice and fair play. You are very intuitive and can have a strong interest for spiritual and psychic matters. You can use this ability to guide yourself and others. You tend to dislike crowds.

Positive: You are agreeable vigilant and philosophical. You are quick, especially in business.

Career: Excellent name for handling finance, banking and sales brokers.

Love: You need a loving and understanding partner.

Negative: You may lack confidence in water or crowded places but you have the ability to overcome this. Working outside of your comfort zone might be a disadvantage. You will do well to stay wherever you feel most confident and comfortable.

Lowest Form: Immoral actions and scandalous activities.

Health: Mental Nerves come with this number but to a lesser degree than 11, 22, 29 and 38. However you are advised to avoid arguments and confrontations because this will result in stress and strain which can affect daily life and your health.

Number 48

(R3)

You like the good life and you can have it.

This definition is balanced or altered by influences from your other names.

You have a fond love for fun and the good things in life. You are quick to learn. You are faithful in partnerships and marriage.

Positive: You are very intuitive, godly and spiritual with potential psychic ability. You can succeed and make things happen without trying. Use this gift wisely and you can attain greatness with ease. Should you fail, you have the drive and ability to get back up and start from nothing all over again. Do not abuse this gift or it will flip the other way and smack you!

Career: Entertainment/amusement industry or any of the arts.

Love: You are very faithful, sincere, passionate and affectionate by nature. You can be successful with your partner in both home projects and business.

Negative: You do not always finish what you start, usually because the project no longer brings the fun and inspiration you need.

Lowest Form: False, disloyal. Seek extravagant material possessions.

Health: Throat.

Number 49

(R4)

Extrovert by number. Intelligent. Open minded.

This definition is *greatly* influenced by your other names/letters/events.

You are very knowledgeable, universally minded, always looking at the big picture. Never too fixed in your ways, always ready and open to making the world a better place. People will listen and follow. Your life is full of changes, usually for the better.

Positive: You are intelligent, sensible, diplomatic and generous. You are very intuitive and will likely have spiritual interests.

Career: You love law and literature. You have excellent leadership ability.

Love: You are helpful, caring and loving.

Negative: Careful or your love for fine wine, cuisine and entertaining can lead to over indulgence.

Lowest Form: Hateful, egotistic and hypocritical.

Health: Circulation of the blood, exercise and avoid fatty foods.

Number 50

(R5)

Mild physical nerves. Active.

Quick to learn. You can have a great life.

This definition is balanced or altered by influences from your other names. Physical nerves are not prominent with this number but can increase with influence from other names.

You have a love of justice and fair play. You love knowledge and literature and you learn quickly simply by looking or listening. You can be an excellent public speaker. You can be generous and love to entertain, cook, wine and dine. You are feisty and active but physical nerves do not rank high with this name unless aggravated by negative conditions.

Positive: This name represents great progress and success. You are fearless yet respectful. You can achieve whatever you set your mind to.

Career: You would make an excellent lawyer or defense attorney.

Love: This name can have many affairs in life and love.

Negative: You can focus too much on work and luxuries. Your love for fine wine, cuisine, entertaining can lead to over indulgence.

Lowest Form: You will become vein and conceited.

Health: Usually good hearing and eye-sight but take care of the eyes and especially the liver/gall bladder.

Number 51

(R6)

Introvert. Great potential, clever, but lack confidence.

This definition is balanced or altered by influences from your other names.

You are quiet often dealing with inner emotions, yet you always put on a smile and talk cheerfully. This name indicates movement or change. Startling occurrences will come with this name. Despite your fears and introvert nature, you can be very successful. You love music and like to sing, even if it is only in your mind.

Positive: You have a talent for languages chemistry physics medicine and abstract science. What you fear the most can become your best subject when you gain confidence.

Career: You can be successful in any area of science or the medical field.

Love: Conditions may prevent marriage, or absence and separation after marriage. You can be passionless, which will do little to promote love.

Negative: You worry too much, even when unnecessary. You can be jumpy, edgy, easily irritated and can have a temper.

Lowest Form: Inner fears promote bad temper.

Health: Heart.

Number 52

(R7)

Skillful, organized, generous,

good natured and intuitive.

This definition is balanced or altered by influences from your other names.

Frequent travel usually comes with this name. You handle problems with prudence, patience and courage. You enjoy work. You love mountains and earth's natural wonders. You can be very intuitive.

Positive: You are skillful capable and punctual. You are strong and physically active.

Career: You can be military minded which opens many career prospects where you can both take or give orders and fulfill your role in a business with precision.

Love: You are generous and good natured.

Negative: Talking too much or getting too deep into people's affairs can get you into trouble. Sometimes your vision and knowledge is beyond others. They will not understand, so close your eyes, shut up when necessary and you will do well.

Lowest Form: Can be very conceited.

Health: The spleen.

Number 53

(R8)

Introvert. Superb attention to small details.

This definition is balanced or altered by influences from your other names.

You are very quiet serious and notice the smallest detail in any object or subject. You like to be calm, in your own space and take life easy. You can get lost in your own thoughts. You can enjoy meditation, abstract science solving puzzles and crosswords.

Positive: You can make steady progress throughout life. Your interest in philosophy and abstract science promotes and develops your open mind.

Career: You are best suited to position of authority, you can excel where great attention to detail is required. You would make an excellent detective.

Love: You need a very open truthful and sincere partner.

Negative: You can be too concerned about other people's business. You do not like or do well with big projects, big expanses, or rapid expansion. You prefer smaller projects where your intricate ability excels.

Lowest Form: You are capable of and very good at spying on people.

Health: Stomach and throat.

Number 54

(R9)

Introvert by number.

A visionary but you can face difficulties.

This definition is balanced or altered by influences from your other names.

You are a fine writer and speaker and possess gentle persuasive powers. You can gain a good reputation with your knowledge and desire to learn.

Positive: You are a visionary. You are good planning. You can cultivate and build with the people. This name will usually live a long life.

Career: You are good in all forms of communication, especially direct face to face with people.

Love: Choose your partner wisely. An early faithful loving marriage will stand you well.

Negative: Problems and difficulties tend to come your way.

Lowest Form: You hate authority, capable of terrorism. Negative influences can make your positives flip and you will become lame.

Health: Take care not to strain the groin area, beware of sexual diseases.

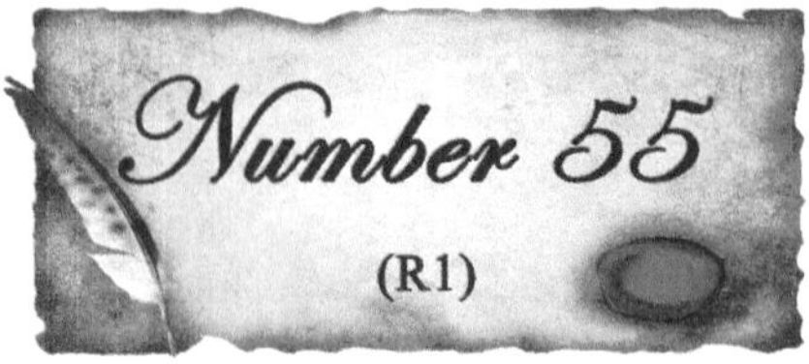

Vitality. Excellent as a minister councilor or healer.

This definition is balanced or altered by influences from your other names.

You are honest and honorable. You will be recognized for your high morals, good intent and fine qualities. This number often has a strong voice, especially when speaking opinions. People will come to you for advice and guidance.

Positive: You are bright intelligent and usually fortunate in money matters.

Career: Your devotion to seeking happiness for all mankind would make you an excellent man of God, a minister, spiritual councilor, healer or advisor.

Love: You are full of life and vitality, so you need an equally physical and equally minded partner.

Negative: This number has a tendency to breaking the right arm.

Lowest Form: With negative balance you can flip and take the wrong path.

Health: Take care of the head and liver.

Number 56

(R11)

Mental Nerves. You may *appear introvert.*

Renown and fortune.

This definition is *greatly* influenced by your other names/letters/ events. Too many names with physical or mental nerves can put this person into overload requiring careful examination.

Your name often brings renown and fortune. Life will be full of changes, especially within your environment. You have a good dry sense of humor. You prefer to not take recognition for your achievements and you can be secretive regarding your methods used to attain success. Your nervous disposition will make you appear introvert.

Positive: You are philosophical, modest, agreeable and usually quiet.

Career: You are ambitious and can do well working on your own. Do not let nervous apprehension slow your progress. You can overcome this obstacle especially with positive influence from other names or events.

Love: You take great care to select only a few close friends. Your quiet reserved nature can bring problems with relationships if you do not open up and share what is troubling you.

Negative: Your nervous disposition and stress can slow your progress. You can lack patience, be extremely blunt and will cut corners if your nerves are not controlled.

Lowest Form: Can be over ambitious.

Health: Nerves relates to stress. Stress can cause many health problems.

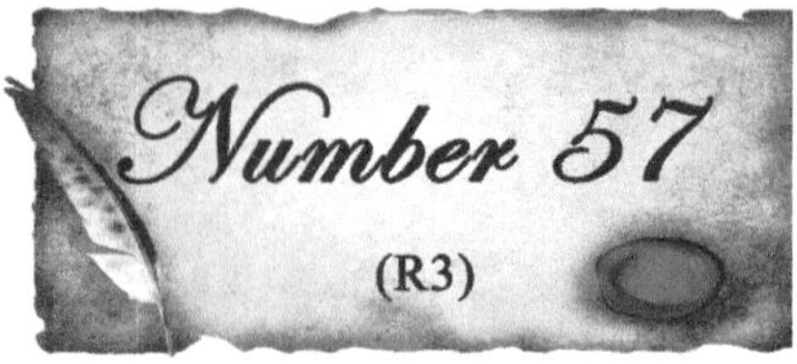

Brilliant kind and successful but you can overdo it.

This definition is balanced or altered by influences from your other names.

Success in business, you can be very prosperous. You can be recognized for your endearing courageous abilities. You will put a lot of effort into projects, business, pleasure or charitable work. You will fight for good causes.

Positive: You are brave, frank, genuine and affectionate with a sweet nature.

Career: Your military obedient mind gives you good prospects. You can excel in any caring profession for business or simply for pleasure.

Love: Take care not fall in love too fast with the wrong partner.

Negative: Too much effort and trying too hard will drain you physically and mentally. Be careful as people will try to take advantage of your kindness.

Lowest Form: Disloyal and not trustworthy.

Health: Throat.

Number 58

(R4)

Extrovert. Good personality

but can be irritable and bad tempered.

This definition is *greatly* influenced by your other names/letters/ events. Pendulum, you can swing good or bad.

You can be good natured with a bright personality. You are brave but not looking for glory. A good leader, people will come to you for help. You like things in order.

Positive: You are honest. You will get straight to the point rather than mix words. You like to help others. Usually calm, realistic and know your abilities.

Career: Success in commerce or as a physician, especially optical.

Love: You need a partner who can respond to your affectionate nature or you will likely seek love elsewhere. Some 58's will have many love affairs.

Negative: You can swing the other way becoming irritable and bad tempered when provoked.

Lowest Form: With the wrong negative balance you become angry wicked and capable of murder. Some will have strong sexual desires.

Health: Usually good health, but take care of eyes and eyesight.

Number 59

(R5)

Physical nerves.

Determined to conquer and beat all odds.

This definition is *greatly* influenced by your other names/letters/ events. Too many names with physical or mental nerves can put this person into overload requiring careful examination.

You are knowledgeable and smart. You are attracted to water, be it sports, boats, commercial shipping or travelling. You are also connected with literature, libraries, printing, or books, even if just for your personal reading pleasure.

Positive: You have a love for speculation. This can be to your advantage if you make the right choices. You can be a global entrepreneur and a very good networker.

Career: Banking, finance or insurance broker. You can have success with boats, shipping or travel.

Love: You have a good heart but do not always find time for love.

Negative: Your desire for speculation can lead to gambling.

Lowest Form: Gambling and debts lead to fraud and swindling.

Health: This number usually has a long life, but take care of your liver and gall bladder. Stress brings nerves and nerves affect your health

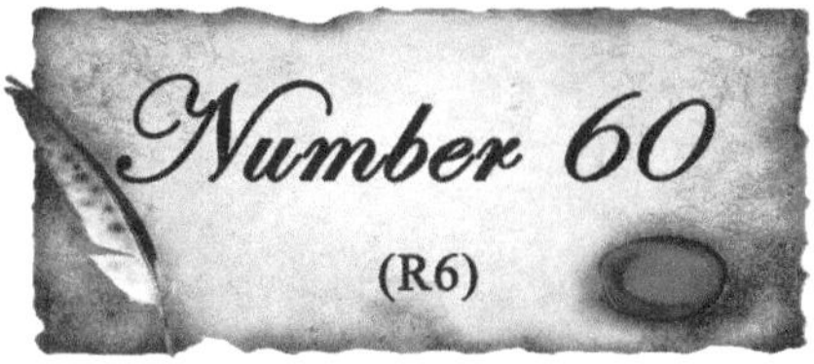

You love to make rules and regulations.

This definition is balanced or altered by influences from your other names.

You are cheerful, very good company and you enjoy friendships. You love to help those less fortunate and will readily aid a sick or dying person. You are meticulous and like to do everything to your best ability.

Positive: You have a love for rules and regulations, giving or making.

Career: Your attention to rules would make you an excellent lawyer, teacher, manager, supervisor or work within police, military or politics.

Love: You have a kind soul. But be careful not to make too many rules.

Negative: Careful your love for rules and regulation does not become an obsession or people will no longer want to be in your company.

Lowest Form: Disobedient to authority. Insubordinate and lack respect.

Health: Heart.

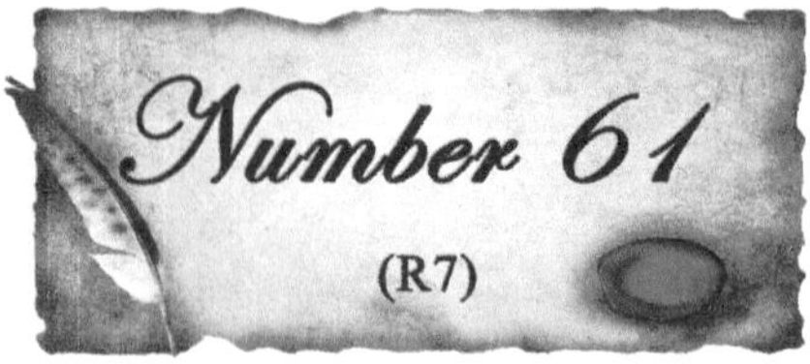

Straightforward sincere nice person

This definition is balanced or altered by influences from your other names.

You love travel, for business or pleasure, short distance or long distance. You enjoy the honest pleasures of life. People will come to you for help and guidance.

Positive: You are sensible and sincere which will bring you many friends. You strive for success patiently but do not seek recognition.

Career: Anything you put your mind to. You are good planning.

Love: You are quiet by nature thus need a partner who can add balance.

Negative: You should rise above and avoid quarrels whenever they come your way.

Lowest Form: Poor judgment, bad decisions, leading to arguments.

Health: Sensitive stomach. Careful what you eat, it may come back up.

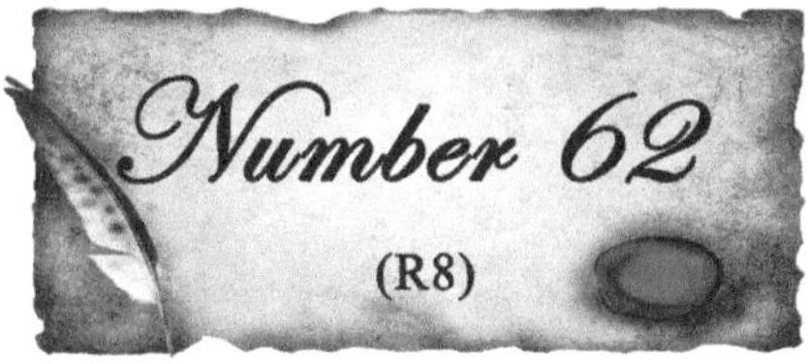

Introvert. Wise with brilliant mind.

You like peace, quiet and solitude.

This definition is balanced or altered by influences from your other names.

You consume knowledge with ease and put it to good use. You would make an excellent pharmaceutical chemist. You are fond of regulations. You must avoid high places if you do not instinctively do so already. You like peace and quiet within a calm environment.

Positive: You are modest, very wise and philosophical.

Career: You can work best within a big organization where you have control in your workplace. You can excel with important small objects or projects requiring exact detail. Big or busy projects do not suit you.

Love: You are not very sociable, often preferring your own company.

Negative: Can be too domineering. Be humble and you will benefit.

Lowest Form: You are not consistent or fun to be with. Expect divorce and loss of friends.

Health: Indigestion or stomach problems.

Number 63

(R9)

Introvert by number.

You are active, industrious and very clever.

This definition is balanced or altered by influences from your other names.

You are a natural reformer and could work well within the church or doing charitable work for pleasure. This number is usually safe from accidents.

Positive: You are subtle, ingenious, industrious and active.

Career: Commerce, banking or physician.

Love: Your introvert nature will benefit from a strong motivating partner.

Negative: You can dream up schemes above and beyond your capacity. You do not always finish what you start which creates disorder.

Lowest Form: You will squander time and money on useless projects.

Health: Usually good health, but avoid physical strain to the groin area and beware of sexual diseases.

Number 64

(R1)

Very sharp but can have over active mind.

This definition is balanced or altered by influences from your other names.

Literature ranks high on your list of favorites, whether reading, writing or simply collecting books. You are precise with detail. You have a very active mind.

Positive: You have a good temperament and enjoy learning. You like to push the barriers to the extreme in search of knowledge and discovery.

Career: Professor, author or literary expert.

Love: This name will often remain single.

Negative: Your attention to detail can make you over critical.

Lowest Form: You will criticize even when your knowledge is limited.

Health: Take care of your lungs and breathing apparatus.

Chapter Eight

PREPARING YOUR EVENTS CHART

The next step is to calculate your events chart and see what positive or negative influences are affecting your life, year by year. This is usually the most exciting part for many. You can confirm what has happened in your past, look at your present and see what is in store for your future. Will you need sun glasses or an umbrella?

There are two potential charts, primary and undertone. You will probably know from Chapters Three and Four, which applies to you. If you do not, then calculate both charts for comparison. I will begin by demonstrating how to calculate a primary chart. First, find a green, red and blue pen. Green is to mark positive letters on your chart. Red is for negative letters and blue is for neutral letters.

At the end of this book, there is a Chapter titled *Work Tools.* You will see three pages with a blank one hundred year events chart together with a primary numbers chart and an undertone numbers chart. You will find it beneficial to copy these and use them for your personal calculations. As mentioned before, if you are calculating several names and especially if you want to create, alter or change names, you will find the work tool programs available on my website offer a huge advantage for both speed and accuracy. www.namesdoctor.com

Let us assume your name is Jack 7, Ian 15, Adams 11. Start with Jack. Using the calculation process of adding together the number for each letter as described in chapter three, Jack totals 7. The J is 1, the A is 1, C is 3 and K is 2. The same numbers reflect the duration of time each letter is active within the chart. So, J lasts for one year, as does A. The C lasts three years and K lasts two years.

Using the blank events chart, start on the top line under the zero, which represents your age at birth. Write the letter J with a green pencil in this box. Then write the A with a blue pencil in the next space which is under the 1. The next letter is C, which is green and is represented by the number 3. Write that letter three times in the next three spaces. K relates to the number 2, also green, so write that letter twice in the next two spaces.

You have filled 7 of the first spaces on the top line with the name Jack. Now, continue again. The J will fall under the 7, because on Jack's seventh birthday, he starts the cycle for this name again. Take a look at the chart below. You can repeat the name Jack indefinitely, for as many years that you need to calculate.

0	1	2	3	4	5	6	7	8	9	10	11	12	13	14	15	16
J	a	c	c	c	k	k	J	a	c	c	c	k	k	J	a	c

Now repeat the same process for Ian and Adams. The formation of letters for each year will look like this.

0	1	2	3	4	5	6	7	8	9	10	11	12	13	14	15	16
J	a	c	c	c	k	k	J	a	c	c	c	k	k	J	a	c
I	I	I	I	I	I	I	I	I	a	n	n	n	n	n	I	I
A	d	d	d	d	a	m	m	m	m	s	A	d	d	d	d	a

You repeat the same process for undertone. Use the undertone numbers chart to evaluate the years applicable to each letter. Jack 29, Ian 21, Adams 34.

The letter J lasts for 8 years as does the A. The letter C is for 6 years and the K is for 7 years. The undertone chart will look like this.

0	1	2	3	4	5	6	7	8	9	10	11	12	13	14	15	16
J	J	J	J	J	J	J	J	a	a	a	a	a	a	a	a	c
I	I	I	I	I	I	I	I	I	a	a	a	a	a	a	a	a
A	A	A	A	A	A	A	A	d	d	d	d	d	a	a	a	a

Earlier in this book, I mentioned adoptions and name change by marriage.

When you take a new name or change your name, for purposes of calculating the chart, you always run the new names starting from age zero. However when you *read* the letter combinations, you only include the new names from the day month and year you formally took those names. You calculate the chart from age zero because it was always in your destiny to have the new names. That's right. You were destined to marry him or her. Your life has already happened. You are merely fulfilling the contract you made with our creator before you came here. This is why premonitions and astrological charts when predicted or calculated by somebody gifted or knowledgeable can be so accurate. The same applies with *Name Reality.*

Here is an example of overlaying a new chart upon name change by marriage.

Let us go back to a previous example. Mary Jo Anderson's mother's maiden name was Smith. She married Michael Jones in 2007 when she was twenty. The individual charts are shown first and then the Jones is overlaid in 2007. The new personality and effect of the letters from Jones changed her life the day she married and took the name of her husband.

1987	1988	1989	1990	1991	1992	1993	1994	1995	1996	1997	1998	1999	2000	2001	2002	2003
0	1	2	3	4	5	6	7	8	9	10	11	12	13	14	15	16
M	M	M	M	a	r	r	r	r	r	r	r	r	r	y	y	y
J	o	o	o	o	o	o	J	o	o	o	o	o	o	J	o	o
A	n	n	n	n	n	d	d	d	d	e	e	e	e	e	r	r
S	m	m	m	m	i	i	i	i	i	i	i	i	i	t	t	h

2004	2005	2006	2007	2008	2009	2010	2011	2012	2013	2014	2015	2016	2017	2018	2019	2020
17	18	19	20	21	22	23	24	25	26	27	28	29	30	31	32	33
y	y	y	y	M	M	M	M	a	r	r	r	r	r	r	r	r
o	o	o	o	J	o	o	o	o	o	o	J	o	o	o	o	o
r	r	r	r	r	r	r	s	o	o	o	o	o	o	n	n	n
h	h	h	h	h	h	h	S	m	m	m	m	i	i	i	i	i

Jones from birth would look like this.

1987	1988	1989	1990	1991	1992	1993	1994	1995	1996	1997	1998	1999	2000	2001	2002	2003
0	1	2	3	4	5	6	7	8	9	10	11	12	13	14	15	16
J	o	o	o	o	o	o	n	n	n	n	n	e	e	e	e	e

2004	2005	2006	2007	2008	2009	2010	2011	2012	2013	2014	2015	2016	2017	2018	2019	2020
17	18	19	20	21	22	23	24	25	26	27	28	29	30	31	32	33
s	J	o	o	o	o	o	o	n	n	n	n	n	e	e	e	e

Add Jones to Mary Jo Anderson Smith at age 20.

2004	2005	2006	2007	2008	2009	2010	2011	2012	2013	2014	2015	2016	2017	2018	2019	2020
17	18	19	20	21	22	23	24	25	26	27	28	29	30	31	32	33
y	y	y	y	M	M	M	M	a	r	r	r	r	r	r	r	r
o	o	o	o	J	o	o	o	o	o	o	J	o	o	o	o	o
r	r	r	r	r	r	r	s	o	o	o	o	o	o	n	n	n
h	h	h	h	h	h	h	S	m	m	m	m	i	i	i	i	i
			o	o	o	o	o	n	n	n	n	n	e	e	e	e

If you are dominant in undertone, any new names you take add or change, will come in with primary energy. You will need to calculate two charts. One undertone with the old names you are keeping and another chart with any new names calculated as primary, then overlay according to the year of change.

The next chapter gives you the meaning and influence of each letter in the alphabet. Chapter Ten explains how to understand the combination of these letters in your chart.

Chapter Nine

LETTERS A to Z

This chapter shows you the influencing forces created by each individual letter of the alphabet for purposes of *Name Reality.* It is not difficult to understand the combined effects in a chart. It is logical. Each letter has a force upon each and every other letter in the table. If one letter in a specific year is positive, it does not guarantee you will see the fullness of that letter. Balance from the other letters is very important. Full consideration must also be given to age and personality when evaluating the meaning of combined letters for any one year. We each deal with life situations in different ways. This part of *Name Reality* requires some practice to fully understand. The notes that follow in the A to Z definitions will help guide you. More advice on letter combinations is shown in the next chapter.

To help you get acquainted with the letters A to Z, and for simplicity, I have included a one-page quick reference guide at the end of this chapter.

When the notes refer to *letters in the chart,* it is directed to the one specific year in question you are analyzing.

Green Letters are Positive. Red Letters are usually Negative.

Blue Letters are influenced by other letters in the table.

Green letters can bring out the Positive in Blue.

Red letters can bring out the Negative in Blue.

A. The letter A indicates activity to all the other letters in the chart for that year. It will make a good chart better and more active in a good direction. A bad chart will thus become more active in a negative direction. One A in a name can add clear-headiness. More than one A in the same name can make you very alert, quick in judgment and active in many areas of your life, for example Sandra. Multiple A's in the same name, can make you over critical, example Samantha. Multiple A's throughout all your names can sometimes make you cynical and sarcastic.

This letter is active for 1 year in a primary chart and 8 years undertone.

B The letter B can be a highly strung or sensitive period of time and has three possible meanings. Your interpretation will depend on which other letters are present in the chart. When this letter is coupled with letters indicating love and romance, it can indicate a serious relationship or marriage sometimes with high expectations. If the other letters indicate stress and strain, then the letter B indicates physical delicacy, or Illness. A closer study of all your health definitions will help locate the potential illness area. Double B in the table can indicate serious health problems, especially to the head. If none of the above, then this letter enhances intuitiveness or indicates spiritual awareness and can enhance any natural psychic ability you may have. Too many B's in your names can increase your intuitiveness and give delicacy to health as they tend to produce an over spiritual mind and body.

This letter is active for 2 years in a primary chart and 7 years undertone.

C The letter C is a vivifying force which indicates good health, strength and recovery especially if previous letters brought illness. In life, the letter C gives you ability to cope with anything. However it has a slight tendency to slow your progress. To advance, one should be humble, not aggressive, when in this letter. In a negative chart, C can indicate throat problems but is not usually harmful unless matched with extreme letter combinations.

This letter is active for 3 years in a primary chart and 6 years undertone.

D The letter D indicates movement and change in your life. Other letters in the table determine if the changes are for the better or for the worse. The changes usually bring expansion into your life often with more responsibility. This letter also indicates travel. More than one D can bring sudden change, often out of your control. Two D's can indicate accidents and extreme cases can be life threatening. Example, L L D D could be death by accident and N N D D could be health related, but H I D D would be the stressful emotional loss of a near relative or close friend.

This letter is active for 4 years in a primary chart and 5 years undertone.

E The letter E always adds Eventfulness or Extremes to all the other letters in the chart. This will make good events better and bad events worse. It exaggerates both highs and lows. It can be tiring if you go from one extreme to another. Two or more E's in the same name can bring extremes to all areas of your life. Too many consecutive E's or 5's can make you impulsive and unpredictable. An example is the name Sweeney. E as an individual letter is 5 (W and N are also a 5) which brings physical nervous energy making it difficult to relax. Sports and mentally demanding physical activities are a good remedy to burn off the excess energy, especially later in life. Try golf.

This letter is active for 5 years in a primary chart and 4 years undertone.

F The letter F indicates concealment or to discover, search and find. Other letters in the chart can to determine the outcome. The letter F can be you concealing things from other people, or other people concealing things from you. It could simply indicate you concealing emotions, worries or concerns. If the letter F is with letters indicating money, you must be careful with all financial matters. If other letters indicate health, take care of the heart. When F is the first letter in one or more of your names, or a short name where the F rotates in your cycle frequently, concealment can be a permanent trait. This can be exaggerated if your names are introvert or have excess mental nervous energy. On a better note, concealment can be your desire to hide or search for items, like an explorer. Forrest Fenn searched for artifacts from an early age. He became a self-made millionaire art dealer and then buried a fortune in gold coins and gems. He left a list of clues of how to find the treasure hoping to encourage kids to explore nature rather than stay at home watching TV and playing video games.

This letter is active for 6 years in a primary chart and 3 years undertone.

G The letter G is **Very Positive** and indicates gains in all areas of your life. The gains can be financial emotional or health. They work best when decisions are made, preferably by you. If decisions are made for or about you, you can still gain, but take care that those acting for you are both knowledgeable and have positive letters in their chart, especially in financial matters. The more decisions you make, the more often you can gain. The bigger the decision, the bigger you gain. However if you don't know you are in this letter you can miss opportunities.

This letter is active for 7 years in a primary chart and 2 years undertone.

H The letter H brings stress and strain. It can be negative and drain you. Sometimes the strain can be striving for pleasure or gain. If other letters in your chart are positive, like G, then the stress and strain can be for a positive result. Similar as H in Harry, 34, a good name for business, can make him strain, wanting to get ahead in life. H with the letter O can put strain on finances and/or health. H with the letter N can put a strain on relationships and health. H D D I in a table would indicate the death of a close friend as personal emotions were involved with nervous strain. Similar as H O I could indicate a broken heart.

This letter is active for 8 years in a primary chart and 1 year undertone.

I. The letter I indicates sharpened personal feelings. You can experience a sensitive time of deep intense emotions. Usually the emotions are mixed. It can make you shy, or bold, but in either case, sympathetic and intuitive. This letter can bring happiness from people who give you happiness. Sadly it can also bring the exact opposite from sad events. You may even experience both emotions at the same time. If this letter couples with an A, then it can indicate a birth or pregnancy for you or somebody close to you. If the letter N begins the following year, the birth will likely be for you. Double I with A can sometimes result in twins. If coupled with the letter U, it can bring losses of relatives and friends. Two or more letter I's in the same name can make you very intuitive and sensitive. Shy with introvert names and bold with extrovert names. In a negative chart you can become over sensitive or aggressive and difficult to be with. The letter I can also indicate love/romance if your names are caring/loving, or from positive letter combinations in the table.

This letter is active for 9 years in a primary chart and 9 years undertone.

J The letter J places you in a position of leadership. This can be in either family or career depending on the other letters in the chart for that year. This will come into your life whether you want it or not. It nearly always results in a gain or advantage. A closer look at the letters following this year can often reveal if it is a leadership within work or home. In a table of negative letters it will result in an unwilling leadership.

This letter is active for 1 year in a primary chart and 8 years undertone.

K The letter K is a vivifying force. In a table showing illness, it will aid recovery. It usually indicates travel and change. Take care as it can scatter your time, money and energy. It can bring nervousness, rashness or apprehension. If with the letter U, then it *confirms* the losses indicated by the letter U. In a good chart it can represent a successful period of expansion, study, learning and advancement.

This letter is active for 2 years in a primary chart and 7 years undertone.

L The letter L indicates change, travel and movement. This can be for both long and short journeys, for business and pleasure. L generally brings better conditions to your most areas of your life including health and recovery. However the change can sometimes be at self-sacrifice, for example, in a good chart, a new better paid job, but far away from family and home. In a negative table the self-sacrifice can increase for the worse. Double L's in a table can flip two ways. 2 L's can double the recovery from bad health. However 2 L's usually indicate accidents and falls. This also applies if you are passing through a single L this year and a double L next year. The letter L lasts for 3 years. The transition from one L to a double L lasts for one year. If this occurs, it gives danger of a physical fall. Stairs, ledges and high windows should be avoided or given the utmost care. 2 L's obviously increase self-sacrifice risks. Double L especially one on top of the other in the table can indicate death. A closer look at the full chart, names, health issues etc. will give a better indication what to avoid. L can indicate the throat in health matters.

This letter is active for 3 years in a primary chart and 6 years undertone.

M The letter M brings change into a person's life. The change will be for the better if the other letters in the table are positive, however the changes will be for the worse if other letters in the table are negative. The letter M also indicates travel. If the letter M and L occur together, then the travel can be long distance. When a chart contains more than one M, the changes can be very sudden, sometimes out of your control, even violent. Double M can result in sudden death, though usually it is a relative that dies.

This letter is active for 4 years in a primary chart and 5 years undertone.

N The letter N represents the physical body and usually indicates love, romance and loving conditions. It can indicate engagement, marriage or similar conditions. Love can also come from children, family or close friends. If this letter is with a T, then marriage or marriage conditions are almost guaranteed. If it couples with U, the romance will likely go nowhere. Two or more N's in the chart can indicate more love, However two or more N's, together with a T or B will usually indicate health issues. N or double N with double D, L, M, O, R, T, U and X need close attention for potential health problems. Two N's, one below the other in a chart, can indicate health. A closer look at your names and other letters in the chart may show what to avoid or take care of. Multiple N's in your names can indicate a lot of love coming to you, from one or many people. If your names are generally positive it can also indicate you can be very caring and loving, returning love towards one or many people.

This letter is active for 5 years in a primary chart and 4 years undertone.

O The letter O indicates money and stability. This can be for better or for worse, depending upon other letters in the chart. It adds slowness to your life, making progress difficult when influenced by negative letters. However it adds stability when influenced by positive letters. One letter O can make you determined. More O's from other names in the chart that year can make you very or extremely determined. Multiple O's in the chart can also make life very slow. The letter O also indicates health to the chest, heart and lung areas. Two or more O's one below another in the chart can indicate health problems towards the chest heart and lungs. Two O's in the chart, but separated by another letter, can indicate two sources of income Two or more O's in the same name or multiple O's in ones names can make you slow in making a decision and sometimes stubborn once decided upon your course. Two O's, one in each of two names, can make you cautious. Too many O's in all your names can make you slow in physical movement. I A O in a chart can indicate a broken heart.

This letter is active for 6 years in a primary chart and 3 years undertone.

P The letter P indicates power and success. However care is needed in as bankruptcy and ruin can follow. The letter P gives a tendency to spend rather than saving. P with a T or B can indicate health issues usually towards the head or brain.

This letter is active for 7 years in a primary chart and 2 years undertone.

Q The letter Q is positive and life giving as it suppresses negative. It influences career, health and travel. If other letters show illness, the letter Q will aid recovery. In business or career it will produce a gain. The letter Q can indicate a successful marriage. On a negative note, Q is usually followed by the letter U. Any problems suppressed by the Q will come out sharply when you begin the letter U.

This letter is active for 8 years in a primary chart and 1 year undertone.

R The letter R indicates much fast action making you busy, active and rushing around. This affects all areas of your life, not just physically, but also mentally and emotionally. It can be tiring, but is not harmful. Two or more letter R's are not good as the effect is doubled or trebled. One R with an A or E exaggerates the effect in a similar way. This can indicate stress, illness and accidents from rushing around too much, or very often, impulsive bad decisions. It can also bring domestic worries and cares into the home and in extreme cases, separation or divorce or problems with or for your parents, especially your father. On a better note, one letter R, can strengthen the mind and body, keeping you alert, similar to the way regular moderate exercise is good. Whereas double R is not good, just like too much exercise is too strenuous. When R is the first letter of a name, it indicates strong imagination or an open mind. Learning becomes easier without fixed ideas. However in a negative name or letter combination, you can also be open to negative thoughts or actions.

This letter is active for 9 years in a primary chart and 9 years undertone.

S The letter S sharpens and protects. In a good table it can make events better. In a negative table it always makes things appear worse than they are but at the same time it protects. You may see problems appear worse for the first half of the year and the second half of the year problems resolve for the better.

This letter is active for 1 year in a primary chart and 8 years undertone.

T The letter T indicates a time of change, maybe a change of home, or change of career. Other letters present in the chart will show if the changes are positive or negative. In a chart showing loving conditions, the T can indicate a serious relationship or marriage. In a chart showing health the letter T indicates the head area. Two or more T's can indicate potential head problems from accidents or illness, example T T B indicates health. T L L in a chart would indicate accident with head injuries. Two or more T's in the same name can indicate head problems from accidents or illness.

This letter is active for 2 years in a primary chart and 7 years undertone.

U The letter U can be Very Negative. It indicates loss. The losses can be financial, emotional, or both. Sometimes other letters in the chart that year or the following year can indicate where to expect the loss. The letter U can lead to missed opportunities in life, especially if U is the first vowel in a name, for example, Ruth. This can include education, business, career, family and love.

This letter is active for 3 years in a primary chart and 6 years undertone.

V The letter V in a negative chart can indicate a weakness in your character. You may find it difficult to say no when others ask too much of you. You could be easily led astray and do things you normally would not. If there are 2 V's in the same year, this will exaggerate the effect, bringing extravagance and loss of money. If the letter U is present, it can indicate financial losses from gambling or speculation. On a better note, in a good chart, the letter V can indicate travel.

This letter is active for 4 years in a primary chart and 5 years undertone.

W The letter W indicates wavering conditions. In a good chart it can indicate travel but will still create ups and downs, though mild depending upon the strength of the other letters in the chart. In a negative chart the wavering conditions can lead to anxiety, worry and self-doubts. This can be draining, affecting all aspects of life including health.

This letter is active for 5 years in a primary chart and 4 years undertone.

X The letter X tends to be negative, making you clumsy or lack coordination, but is very dependent upon influence from other letters in the chart. When negative, this can extend to danger of falls, injuries and accidents, especially from moving vehicles.

This letter is active for 6 years in a primary chart and 3 years undertone.

Y The letter Y is **Very Positive**. It brings success to all areas of your life. Y gives safety on or around water and for travel. Y is good for health and aids recovery if there is sickness.

This letter is active for 7 years in a primary chart and 2 years undertone.

Z This letter is positive for control and repression. It can put you in a strong position where you are managing people or taking control of situations. In health this letter aids recovery as it represses. Together with the letter N, it can indicate very strong love, romance or marriage.

This letter is active for 8 years in a primary chart and 1 year undertone.

Green letters are Positive. Red letters are usually Negative.

Blue Letters are influenced by other letters.

Green letters can bring out the Positive in Blue.

Red letters can bring out the Negative in Blue.

A: Adds activity to all other letters.

B: Intuitive, sensitive or highly strung. Stress=illness. N=marriage. Beware 2xB health.

C: Control, strong health with the ability to cope. Very Positive.

D: Change, expansion, more responsibility. Travel. Beware 2xD accidents.

E: Extremes. Good things Better, Bad things Worse.

F: Concealment by you or towards you. To discover, search and find.

G: Gains in all areas. Very Positive.

H: Stress and Strain. Not always negative, can be strain or striving for gain.

I: Exaggerates Emotions. Highs and lows.

J: Leadership in Family or Career.

K: Change. Travel. Strong health. Period of Learning. Apprehension when negative.

L: Change Advancement Travel. Beware 2xL accidents, self-sacrifice.

M: Change Travel Beware 2xM can be dangerous.

N: Love and Romantic Conditions. Very Positive Sometimes 2xN indicates health.

O: Money and Stability. Beware 2xO health or very slow.

P: Power and Success but beware of spending.

Q: Very Positive for Career Health and Travel.

R: Busy Active Rushing around Beware 2xR = overactive/accidents/illness/family.

S: Sharpens for better or worse but improves.

T: Home or Career Change Beware 2xT head area.

U: Losses—Financial, Emotional or Health. Can be very negative.

V: Can weaken your character, but often brings travel.

W: Wavering conditions. Anxiety, worry and self-doubts. Travel in a good table.

X: Clumsy or accident prone. Very dependent upon other letters in the chart.

Y: Success in all areas. Very Positive.

Z: Controls and Represses. Promotes your people skills.

Chapter Ten

UNDERSTANDING YOUR NAME AND LETTER COMBINATIONS

Reading your name and letter definitions one by one-will give you an indication to who you are and which way your life is heading. If your life is relatively smooth and mostly stress free, you can use this information to make adjustments and know when to take an umbrella if your events chart shows bad weather coming your way. Some personalities clearly show you may have problems with self-confidence, bad temper, anxiety, worries, fears and even phobias. These are easy to recognize. However, in the case where you read your name definitions and do not see obvious problems, the answers can be hidden in the balance of your names, the balance of letters in your chart, or both. Balance can bring out the best or the worst.

NAME COMBINATIONS

Let's start with your names. I wrote the 64 name personalities with the positive indications at the top of the page and the negative comments and lowest form comments at the bottom of the page. All 64 name personalities have both good and bad to varying degrees. Some are extreme. Every personality can flip one way or the other. Everybody has the potential to be a nice person.

How many times have you heard *"he is such a nice boy, I cannot understand why he did that."* The answer is, he did it because his names lack balance, which brings out the negative-or in extreme cases-the lowest form. A poor balance of names can create a monster, as you will see later in this book. It is no accident that some people become drug addicts, alcoholics, suffer depression, have violent tendencies and will even take another's life.

The most common factor to upset your balance is names with nerves. Names with physical or mental nerves are clearly marked at the top of the 64 personality pages in chapter seven. Too many names, primary or undertone, with physical nerves or mental nerves, will put your balance on a knife edge.

This can make you flip from good to bad, for a minute, an hour, a day, a week or permanently. Excess nerves, with names that do not enhance balance, together with poor letter combinations in your chart, will increase negative traits and can activate the lowest form in one or more of your names.

Nerves do not have to mean you are a nervous wreck. Excess nerves can show in something as simple as biting your nails, shaking your leg or tapping your foot when waiting around, anxious with nothing to do.

One name with nerves is usually good because it can give you some spark and often brings with it some intelligence. Two, especially in your primary names can become border line if not balanced or toned down by other names with tranquil qualities. Three nervous names are pushing the boundaries. I had four, two primary and two in my undertone.

When young, you are naturally physically and mentally on the go, so you tend to burn up excess energy. As you age, you naturally slow down. The energy is still there but has nowhere to go. This creates nervous unrest. Some people turn to drugs or alcohol as a temporary escape to relax. Some people naturally keep busy mentally or they keep active physically to stay balanced. Some people lose their minds when they retire because their mental energy is no longer being consumed with brain activity. Some people develop nervous physical disabilities, some implode and some explode. This can be attributed to your emotional state, which usually shows in the balance of your names. Chapters Thirteen and Fourteen have detailed examples and will help you understand how one name can be toned down by another and what can push people into overload.

One primary name with physical nerves and another with mental nerves is not quite as volatile as two names with mental nerves. Two names with physical nerves are usually by a small margin not as volatile as two names with mental nerves.

Names with high activity, 1, 10 19, 28, 37, 46, 55 and 64 will not calm down names with nerves, especially mental nerves as these numbers indicate a quick mind. They can bring out brilliance in a positive combination or aggravate a negative combination. Numbers that will help tone down nerves in some situations are 3, which is good for control, and 30, which is also good for control, relaxation and stress free. The relaxed number 24 trusts everything will work out well. Numbers 6 and 15 seek peace and tranquility. Number 41, although very active, usually gives you good control of your emotions.

Introvert and extrovert is a not a good mix, but it is not harmful. You may be extrovert one minute or one day, and then an introvert the next minute or the next day. It may be confusing for your friends when you, the life and soul of a party, do not want to play one day, yet will the next.

One or especially two names with nerves, mixed together with introvert and extrovert, are when problems can begin to show in a negative direction. The exception is if you have constructive interests that keep you occupied and motivated or other names that help to accomplish this. Otherwise this can be a dangerous mixture that brings out the lowest form in some or all of your names.

For example numbers 5, 11, 14, 16, 22 and 38 can be extrovert and have excess mental or physical nerves. Add introvert from 9, 18, 27, 36, 45, 54 and 63 and you need to pay special attention as mentioned above. Add a 4, 13, 31, 40 or 58 into the mix and the quick temper normally associated with these names, can become violent. Then there are the abnormal numbers like 39, highly sexual and capable of murder. This number needs to be given special attention but *only when in a negative combination.* Again, examples in Chapters Thirteen and Fourteen will help you understand combinations more clearly.

One or two names with nerves, mixed with other names that indicate a lack of confidence or worry, stress and strain, can exaggerate the problems and bring about depression. Needless to say, in some cases, alcohol or drugs become a temporary fix if you do not have the motivation to keep your head above water. If your chart shows positive letters, this can bring some relief. However, when the letters change, you can fall back into seriously difficult times if your letter combinations are negative.

You can calculate how much nerves you are getting from your individual names, both primary and undertone. The more a number with mental or physical nerves defines your character, the more impact you will get from the nerves. In the unlikely event you have highlighted everything written on that personality description page, you will get a full 100% shot of nervous energy. If only half the definitions represent your character then you will likely get a 50% shot of nervous energy from this name.

I have seen a situation where a good friend highlighted only 15% of an undertone page. In this case it was number 29. The nerves reflected from that number were correspondingly low. This showed very much in this person's stable character, especially as the dominant primary number for the same name was 34.

An average percentage number split that I frequently see for primary and undertone is 66% primary and 33% undertone. I sometimes use this number as a quick reference guide, but do not take it for granted as no two people are the same.

Another factor that must be considered is how many names you have. Picture a round birthday cake that needs to be shared equally amongst your friends. The more friends you have, the smaller each piece becomes. The same applies to your names. You are the combination of all your names. The more names you have, the amount each individual name will affect you reduces. One negative name out of 3 is going to have more impact than one negative name in 5.

The same mathematics applies to the affects from each letter in your chart.

LETTER COMBINATIONS

When you attempt to calculate the effects of letters in your own chart, you will find it relatively easy. By now, you should know yourself well enough and understand how you react to different situations. When reading the letters for another person, you must evaluate that person's character before you attempt to understand the effects the letters will have.

If two people have the same combination of letters in any one year of a chart, the interpretation will most likely be very different. Age must be factored into the equation. Lifestyle and the way you react changes as you progress through life. If one person is vibrant and extrovert with a good business mind and the other is introvert with signs of insecurity, the difference will be very significant and clear to see. Positive letters alone do not guarantee happiness.

When somebody has a sensitive balance of names, perhaps with excess nerves, insecurity problems or violent tendencies, problem letter combinations in their chart will affect them much more drastically than someone who has a tranquil balance of names. Again, examples are shown in chapters thirteen and fourteen with well-known personalities that you can relate to.

Within my descriptions of the alphabet letters A to Z, there are notes about the effects created by some combinations. What you must remember most of all when reading your chart is that each letter has a force upon each and every other letter. If you have four letters in your chart for a given year, each one will affect the other three. With a little practice it is easy. Practice on your chart and then move onto somebody you know well before tackling a stranger.

Another useful guide when evaluating a name, combined names or reading a chart is the effects of vowels. I's need A's to make them see more clearly and O's to render them less impulsive. A's need O's to help keep them from being too hasty and O's are always improved by the quickening qualities of A's. The letter E adds extremes or nervousness. This can be good in a positive name or in a positive chart, but can be damaging in a negative chart. Too many E's in a name can make the person very nervous, edgy or erratic. The letter U is for loss and can indicate missing out on opportunities, especially when U is the first vowel in a name.

It is easy to understand if your chart has a lot of red letters (negative), you could be in for a rough ride. Green letters (positive) are a good sign, but do not guarantee a smooth year if matched with a difficult combination of blue letters. I see more problems created by negative combinations of blue letters than simply red negative letters alone. Two or three of the same blue letters can be very negative. The same applies with two of the same red letters. It doubles the negative. Some combinations as described in Chapter Nine can be dangerous.

Always use the full A to Z descriptions. The short one page version is there to help familiarize you with the letters and is good for a quick reference.

If two names in the chart start with new letters in the same year, it will be an important year. If three or more names start with new letters in the same year, it will be a significantly important year.

Letter combinations can run into the billions and cannot be categorized or listed in any way. It is up to you or the person analyzing your name to use skill and judgment. You will find more tips in Chapter Thirteen.

Chapter Eleven

SUMMARY AND CONCLUSIONS FOR PART ONE

At this point in the book, I hope you are beginning to understand how much names affect your life. Your names strongly influence your character and the letters that create your events chart, can make life better or worse, year by year.

A good or bad start in life creates mental impressions that stay with you for the rest of your life. Surroundings and circumstances, especially during childhood, play a major role in the development of your life. There are some truly great people who came from humble or challenging backgrounds and some truly awful people who had everything at their disposals.

Research shows that in most cases it was the balance of each person's names and letters that determined who would advance and who would not. Some names have a strong character and some do not. Some letter combinations can provide a helping hand and some can set you back.

Your life pathway or astrological path is fixed from the very second you are born. Everyone's pathway has doors on each side, left and right, thousands of doors stretching down a long corridor. Behind some doors there is good and behind others there is bad. It is up to you which doors you choose to enter.

You can open a door, take a peek, decide not to go in and close it, or you can go through that door and immerse yourself there for as long as you like. You can go through a doorway for a few seconds, a few months or a few years. You can decide to totally skip one door and move on to another. Regardless which doors you choose, you always come back to the same path, your astrological path, before moving on to another door.

If your names and letter combinations are balanced, it is most likely you will know to stay away from some doors that simply don't feel right. You will move on to other doors that you instinctively know have good things waiting for you on the other side. This will apply to people you know who never seem to worry about anything. They mostly get ahead and are happy with their life regardless of their status, wealth, education or material assets.

When your names lack balance and especially when you are in negative letter combinations, you will likely choose the wrong doors, over and over. When you are in this negative mode, nothing in life will appear to go well. It will feel like you are locked behind a negative door and somebody threw away the key. Life becomes a downward spiral because you then begin to anticipate the worst before it has even happened, leading you towards more negative doors. This will apply to people you know who always worry and complain about everything in life. Generally, they are not happy and their lives are full of sadness, stress or anger. If they had ambition or goals, it is likely they are exhausted from trying and have sunk into a low with little hope of recovery. Very often they have given up and conceded that *this is how it is and it is not going to get any better.*

Self-help gurus will tell you it is all in your mind and that you need a more positive attitude. Speak positive, think positive and visualize positive. They are correct. However, what they do not know or understand is that you can have a brick wall in front of you created by your names. This wall can be anything from a speed bump to the Great Wall of China. This wall can be there temporarily if created by your *letter* combinations. It can be there permanently if created by your *name* combinations.

You can slip over a series of speed bumps or step over a low wall. It might slow your progress but it will not stop you from getting to your destinations. Sometimes, if the wall is too high to climb over, you can, with perseverance, find a way to walk around it. If the wall cannot be passed, you will need a ladder to ascend one side and a rope to descend down the other side. If you do not have a big ladder and a long rope, you might as well be in a canoe floating down the Old Suwannee River without a paddle. You will have no control over the direction of your life. No matter how hard you try, you will not get ahead.

Awareness is the key. Depending upon how much strength you have and how severe your name and letter combinations are, when you know the root of your problem, with help and good direction, very often you can make adjustments to compensate. If this does not work, you cannot change your astrological path, but you do have another option. You can change or modify your name. The chapters that follow show you how to remove brick walls or bumps in the road, enabling you to reach your destination, quickly and comfortably.

Name Reality shows you how to get the best from your astrological chart.

Part Two
Take it to the next level.

Chapter Twelve

REDUCE NUMBERS FOR QUICK CALCULATION

Mathematics is the basis of this system. Using reduced numbers is a good way to quickly determine if a person's names have balance. I must stress this is for quick calculation purposes only. However, it will show you where you need to focus your attention and give you an indication to the person's overall character.

Reduced numbers for every personality 1 to 64 are shown on the top of each page. How you reduce numbers was explained in Chapter Three.

Reduced numbers are 1, 2, 3, 4, 5, 6, 7, 8, 9, 11, and 22. Numbers 11 and 22 are the only two numbers that do not reduce to a single digit.

For example, take personalities 13, 31, 40, 49, and 58. They all reduce to the number 4. Personality number 4 can be considered the root or base from which the other numbers originated, let's call it *the mother number*. Hence, *related numbers* 13, 31, 40, 49, and 58 have some similarities to the *mother number* 4. On the next page, I have listed these similarities for each number, 1 to 9 plus 11 and 22. If you study these and begin to get familiar with each personality for the *mother numbers*, you will quickly learn to assess people by their *related number* combinations. Remember this is a guide. Ultimately, to make an accurate assessment you must read the *related* numbers for that person's names. Do not overlook the *abnormal numbers*, 16, 18, 20, 23, 36, 39, 42, 51, 54 and 58 that can sometimes bring negative influence when aggravated by excess physical or mental nerves or negative letter combinations in the person's chart.

You can calculate a person's overall character based on his primary numbers. As 95% of the population is dominant in primary, it is safe to initially assume and calculate your subject as primary. In the event the person is dominant in undertone, it will likely show up quickly. Undertones were explained in chapter four. Undertone numbers reflect upon the primary number by adding or subtracting strengths or weaknesses. You use the undertone numbers as secondary information to add more content to the character pattern you have already established from the primary numbers. If the person is dominant in undertone, then you read that set of numbers first to determine their overall character. You will see examples at the end of this chapter.

1/. Numbers that reduce to one are **1, 10, 19, 28, 37, 46, 55 and 64.** ***Very energetic quick or active***, some are extrovert and good making money.

2/. Numbers that reduce to two are **2 and 20 only**. Other numbers reduce to 11. ***Quick brain***, usually quiet and gentle. Good eye for detail and well mannered.

3/. Numbers that reduce to three are **3, 12, 21, 30, 39, 48 and 57.** ***Very caring***, energetic and fun to be with. Good control of life and situations.

4/. Numbers that reduce to four are **4, 13, 31, 40, 49 and 58.** ***Extrovert & Pendulum***. Can swing one way or another, good or bad. Can be open minded or empty minded. May oppose rule. Like attention. Can have a temper.

5/. Numbers that reduce to five are **5, 14, 23, 32, 41, 50 and 59.** ***Physical nerves*** 5, 14, 23, 59. Less nerves with 32, 41, 50. Fast paced.

Logical and optimistic. Talkative. Intelligent. For rule and order when positive.

6/. Numbers that reduce to six are **6, 15, 24, 33, 42, 51 and 60.** ***Artistic***, tend be quiet. Appreciate peace and harmony. Some are introvert.

7/. Numbers that reduce to seven are **7, 16, 25, 34, 43, 52 and 61**. ***Executive business type***, good communicating. Like work and making money.

8/. Numbers that reduce to eight are **8, 17, 26, 35, 44, 53 and 62**. ***Very friendly and talkative***. Can be good with detail and small projects, not so good with big projects. Always striving but like peace and quiet to relax.

9/. Numbers that reduce to nine are **9, 18, 27, 36, 45, 54 and 63**. ***Introvert, intuitive and clever***. Like to study and share knowledge. Forgive and forget. Some can lose focus, become dreamy and worry needlessly.

11/. Numbers that reduce to eleven are **11, 29, 38, 47 and 56**. ***Excess nerves and a sensitive brain***. Volatile, can swing very good or very bad. Very active mind with great energy and vitality, or can have nervous outbursts.

22/. Numbers that reduce to twenty two are **22 only.** ***Excess nerves and a sensitive brain***. Does not reduce below 22 but like 4 and 11 has pendulum similarities. Capable of great achievement or great disaster.

4, 11 and 22 are probably the most extreme and volatile of the 64 numbers. All three are the only numbers to have both a highest form and a lowest form. 4 is the opposite of 9 and can clash. Where 4 needs restraint, 9 needs a push.

Quick Guide to Health. Always read the original number for exact information.

1/. Lungs / breathing, except 28 & 37 add head problems. 55 head and liver only.

2/. 2 and 20. **Brain,** fever, headaches, head problems. 20 add food poisoning.

3/. Throat.

4/. Blood circulation, except 58 eyes and sight only.

5/. Liver/gall bladder, nerves or active/energetic, except 50 add sight.

6/. Heart, except 15 add liver and 33 add throat.

7/. Digestion/Stomach except 7/25/52 is spleen and 16 is mental nerves/ brain.

8/. Stomach/digestion. Number 44 add circulation, 53 add throat. All eights have an additional risk of growths, tumors or cancer.

9/. Stomach/digestion and groin, except 54 and 63 are genital area only.

11/. Mental nerves. Number 29 add brain problems.

22/. Mental nerves and brain.

Sensitive Abnormal Numbers that do not follow reduced tradition.

16/. Money or problems bring stress, nerves and affect the brain.

18/. Lose focus if other names do not balance. Dreamy and unlucky.

20/. Negative thoughts can bring about lack of confidence

23/. Worry and stress, sometimes unfortunate.

36/. Some go about things the wrong way and lose out. Often unlucky.

39/. Successful but can face difficulties. Can be sexual and capable of murder.

42/. Good intentions but struggle with negative influence.

51/. Potential talent but lack confidence.

54/. Visionary but can face difficulties.

58/. Good personality but a pendulum 4. Can be sexual and capable of murder.

Please note: the following examples are an exercises based on personalities only with no consideration given to the letters that create the events chart.

As I have said before, happy people rarely do bad things. I have seen people with name combinations that may appear dangerously on the edge, yet they do not show any signs of leading a bad or immoral life. This is because their charts have positive letter combinations creating happy and positive events. The same goes the other way-when-what appears to be a reasonably balanced name combination, is spoiled by negative letter combinations. This will make some years very difficult for what would normally be happy go lucky people.

The world of entertainment showcases many lifestyles. High profile people have very little privacy. The highs and lows of their lives are made public. Some achieve fame and fortune yet live stressful unhappy lives. Alcohol and drug addiction with frequent trips to rehab fill the news every week. Others take their God given gift and flourish, sharing happiness with others less fortunate. When you grasp the basics of this chapter, you will clearly see why so many people go into overload. It shows, every time, in their names.

Balance comes in many numerical forms. The simplest example is taking one each of the reduced numbers and leaving out the numbers that conflict.

Example;1, 2, 3, 4, 5, 6, 7, 8. (9, 11 and 22 are purposely not included)

7/2 + 4/5 + 8/1 + 3/6

The same numbers but undertone dominant would look like this.

2/7 + 5/4 + 1/8 + 6/3

With these numbers, I have purposely deleted the number 9. When the 4 is a primary number, it would not mix well with the 9. For example, if the birthday for this combination were the 9th, it would not necessarily be dangerous, but would add some confusion as the owner would switch from introvert to extrovert.

If the birthday for the first set of numbers were the 11th or 22nd, it would add some spark and change the balance considerably, but would not set off any alarm bells unless the letter chart was negative.

If we move to the second set of numbers where the undertone numbers are dominant, again a 9 for the birthday could be difficult as some 5's tend to be extrovert. If the birthday was the 11th or 22nd, this would also trigger some alarm bells because some 5's have excess physical nerves which, when combined with the mental nerves from 11 and 22, could put this person close to the borderline where problems might arise unless their letter chart was positive.

Another way to look at balance is to picture in your mind a see saw. Yes, that long plank with a pivot in the middle. You might remember when you were a kid, if a bigger heavier child was on the other end you did not have balance. So you were always stuck up in the air unless the heavy child moved closer to the middle, *to level the balance.*

If your numbers were 5/4, 3/6, 6/3, 4/5 and you were born on the 1st you would likely be very active from the 1 but would have good balance. Put the 1 in the middle as the pivot.

5/4 + 3/6 (1) 6/3 + 4/5

In theory, just looking at all the reduced numbers only, none clash. The numbers with nerves, 5, are within the maximum for safety, one primary and one undertone The 3's with 6's will add control and calmness. The weight comes out fairly even on both sides of the see saw.

Too many of the same numbers will indicate lack of balance. This is not harmful unless excess nerves and abnormal numbers come into the mixture. Too many of the same number will double or triple the tendencies of that personality if not balanced by another number. For example, numbers that reduce to 1 are active. Somebody with personalities 10 and 37 which both reduce to a 1 would likely be overactive. If they had one or two numbers that reduce to a 6, representing peace and tranquility, like 15 or 24, this would tone down or help balance with the 10 and 37. Similar to analyzing letters in a chart, each number has a force upon each and every other number. If you have 4 names, each one will affect the other three.

A person with numbers 9/9, 3/6, 3/6 born on the 6th will likely be introvert from the 9's and some 6's can be introvert. Three 6's will make this person artistic and appreciative of peace and harmony. He will be in control of his life or maybe too controlling with other people because he has two of the number 3.

Somebody with 4/5, 1/8, 4/5 born on the 31st will likely have a very extrovert character (2x4), be either mentally or physically active (1), good with detail (8) and intelligent (5). This person will likely have an open mind (31), but a quick temper (2x4).

If your numbers were 5/4, 11/7, 22/5, 4/5 and you were born on the 9th, pray!

From the previous notes, you should know that 4 and 9 are not a great mix. However when added to excess nerves from 11, 22 and the 5 repeating twice, you have a volatile mixture no matter how you arrange the numbers on the see-saw.

When you compare numbers 3/6, 7/2 and 5/4 with 3/6, 7/2 and 9/9, it is clear to see the first set with 5/4 would make the person very active and outgoing.

Where-as the second set with 9/9 would make the person more reserved. The birthday number for either would become a major factor.

On the first page of this chapter, I talked about how to obtain an overall view of somebody's personality based on his primary numbers, assuming he is dominant in primary. I would like to give you an example of how this view can alter quite dramatically if the same person were dominant in undertone.

Let's consider an imaginary person with numbers 22/32, 18/45, 42/30, born on the 12th. The reduced numbers are 22/5, 9/9, 6/3 and 6.

Looking at the primary combination, first we have excess mental nerves from 22. The number 22 and 9 do not go well together. The pendulum 22 is extrovert and capable of great achievement or great disaster. The 9, introvert, especially when an 18, can bring out the worst if this person does not have constructive interests. The 18 is not the best of the 9's as 18 needs focus and concentration to stay on top. The 22 will likely want to wander bringing loss of focus and concentration. Then because the 6 is a 42, an abnormal number that tries to be good but often fails, this person will likely do just that, fail. The sweet and loving 12 will at best have people taking advantage of his kind nature, or worst, make this person overly sexual. This person could be tempted to lead an immoral life. The exception being motivating circumstances created by positive letters in his chart creating success and happiness perhaps with work, hobbies or interests within his social life. Happy people rarely do bad things.

Looking at the undertone combination, you will see a completely different picture. The 5 in this case does not have excess physical nerves because it is 32, very active and sociable with an attractive personality. The 9 is introvert and intuitive. The 45 does not lack focus like 18 and is thoughtful, organized, caring and prepared. The 3 is very caring, energetic and fun to be with. Number 30 is stress free with good control of life and situations.

30 is open minded and can see the big picture. The birthday number 12 is also very kind, caring and loving. My one reservation is this person may be too kind and caring. Meaning some people will take advantage of their sweet nature if this person does not use the control ability they have from the 30.

Now, try changing the birth day to 31. The primary set will likely become a problem with the birth date bringing out the temper and violence from 4 in 31. This person may be empty minded from the 31 as both 22 and 4 have a pendulum affect making it easy for this person's character to swing one way or another.

If the undertone combination is dominant, the temper might be there but more contained to the person being angry with them-self as the overall character is much more relaxed and reserved with the 30 and 45. Also, remember the 3 and 30 gives control so the excess nerves and pendulum from the 22 being an underlying personality has less impact. The 31 will likely make this person very open minded in a positive direction but with a tendency to be extrovert one day and introvert the next. The 31 by number is extrovert and swings like a pendulum which may conflict with the introvert 45. However, the 45 is one of the least introvert of the nine's and as there are no excess nerves provoking the balance, I see no harm resulting from this combination as long as the letter chart is good.

If the birthday were changed to the 11th or 14th then the primary combination will suffer with more nerves putting them into potential overload. The undertone combination will begin to show problems because the additional nerves can potentially bring this person closer to the edge.

You can experiment with birthday numbers 1 to 31 for both the primary and undertone number combinations. You will see how one number can sometimes change everything. This is why each and every one of us is so different.

Again, I must stress that you cannot define a person's personality totally by reading their numbers only. It will serve as a useful guide. You must look at the letters chart to see what influences are happening year by year.

I have seen people with a reasonable balance of names have a poor life because the letters in their chart brought stress, worry and strain from an early age, which then repeated spasmodically throughout their lives every time negative letters repeated in their chart.

A good start in life is very important. The early years create a lasting impression.

UNDERSTANDING THE RELATION OF PRIMARY AND UNDERTONE

Staying with our same imaginary person, 22/32, 18/45, 42/30, born on the 12th, I will now demonstrate how undertone numbers affect primary numbers. They can add strength or weakness.

We have already established that the primary combination has a potential to wander and can be a bit of a rogue, whereas the undertone is a more happy and reserved character.

Looking at the primary combination, the 22 has 32 as an undertone. The 22 will gain some advantage with the 32 as this number is smart with a good memory. However, 32 is very sociable which will likely make this pendulum 22 want to spend more time having fun than working, especially if they lose focus.

The numbers 18 and 45 are both 9 and introvert. Nines always have an undertone of nine. This is a good example where it is very important to read the full *related* number and not rely on the *mother* or reduced number.

The number 18 is a weak character compared to the 45. So when the 18 is primary, the 45 will give it a helping hand by adding some strength. The personality 18 says, sometimes this name is unlucky or plans just do not work out. To keep on track or get back on track, it is very important for you to focus. When sad, you can feel very low and want to be in your own space. The 45 reads, you are thoughtful, caring, organized and prepared.

Next, we have 42 and 30. These two numbers are totally different. The 42 is an *abnormal* number. It can swing one of two ways, either incredibly beautiful or plagued with problems. This number says, with balance, you can be a truly wonderful person, always seeking peace and harmony for all, a beautiful soul. Or, the negative balance from other names and negative events can at best create a difficult life or at worst an immoral and destructive or self-destructive life. The 30 is a good number for control and ability to shrug off stress. The 30 will add some strength in a positive way to the 42. However, considering we already have 22 and 18, I do not see this combination bringing out the best in 42. Unfortunately, the 42 will most likely work against this person unless there are exceptionally good letter combinations in the chart to bring positive events and happiness.

The birthday is 12 and, as you already know, there is no undertone for this number in *Name Reality.*

Now take a look at the name from the other way around where the undertone is dominant. We have already established this is a much happier and relaxed personality.

The 32 will likely fair quite well with the 22, but again beware of the tendency to get carried away with too much emphasis on social life. The 45 will take a small hit and lose some strength by possibly having to deal with one or two of the negatives from 18. But again, this would depend upon the events chart. If the chart was positive, the 18 would cause very little disruption, and vice versa.

The 30 would most likely benefit from the 42 unless there were multiple years of negative influences created by the events chart.

This chapter is probably the most difficult to comprehend and absorb quickly. I suggest you move on to the next chapter but come back when you feel ready to go through these numbers again.

Chapter Thirteen

UNDERSTANDING PEOPLE

To help you analyze the lives of famous names, I will start by giving you some additional information and examples to get you ready.

Initials of names should be read as an important item. They influence the first years of your life and can have a lasting effect. For example, the letter R, when used as the first letter in a name, will make this person open minded. The letter H can make the person strain, sometimes for the better if wanting to get ahead and succeed, or to stress when life is not going well. The letter T can indicate the head or brain and P can indicate power and success. You will see an example in this chapter of a man called Tito Rodolfo Palacio Henry. He fits this description very well, just from his initials. You will find all of these letter descriptions in Chapter Nine, A to Z.

In Chapter Ten, I referred to the effects of vowels. Examples on the next page demonstrate. I's need A's to make them see more clearly and O's to render them less impulsive. A's need O's to help keep them from being too hasty and O's are always improved by the quickening qualities of A's. Those with A's in their names are quick in judgment and very clear headed. With too many A's they can become over critical. Excessive A's will make people cynical and sarcastic.

Too many of the letter E can produce nervousness with daily extremes running from high to low. Many years ago I knew a man named Steven Sweeney. He had a happy home life and a successful business. Yet he found life too stressful and went through a serious nervous breakdown when everybody thought he was doing well. The letter W and the letter N are *related* to the letter E. Both have the number 5, which represents physical nerves. It is not difficult to see, Steven was overloaded with too many successive E's or 5's in his name. The slightest provocation from surroundings or his events chart put him into overload.

If you know people who have a quantity of I's in their names, you will likely find them to be over sensitive or *touchy* but quickly sympathetic with others. Sometimes they will be aggressive or the complete opposite and will become shy, depending upon other letters that make up their names. However, their personal quality will stand out. They are seldom cowards.

The letter O can make a person determined. Too many O's will make a person so determined they may become obstinate and likely slow about making a decision, though immovable once decided. With an excessive amount of O's, this person can be slow in physical movement.

The letter U is for loss and can indicate missing out on opportunities, especially when U is the first vowel in a name.

Early instruction in this book taught you how numbers for letters are reduced to a single digit hence J reduces from 10 to a 1. Now that you are more familiar with the system of *Name Reality*, I can tell you more on this without adding confusion. The original number for letters relating to 1 through 26 or A to Z, do have *some relation* to the same personality number. It is important that you understand that this is additional information and do not stray from the A to Z written definitions. For example, the letter K originally is an 11 before reducing to a 2. You will see that the letter K, even though it is a strong positive letter-does, in a negative table, have a tendency towards nerves, rashness or apprehension. If you read personality number 11 you will see the similarity. The same is evident with all the letters of the alphabet relating to their original number and personalities 1 to 26. The H is an 8. The personality 8 is always striving to get ahead. The P is 16, often successful in business but with a tendency towards overspending. I use this additional information only when I am looking very deep into a name, especially if there are serious problems that need to be addressed.

The name Margaret totals to personality number 38. This number represents bright and intelligent, not one to mince words, and likely to speak the plain truth. She can be spiritual or religious and generous but with a tendency to be extravagant. She will be extremely clear headed from the two A's and an E.

Let's compare the name Margaret with different last names. Margaret Walters (26), Margaret Johnson (32) and Margaret Smith (24). They will each have in a general way the traits of Margaret, nevertheless each will be quite different and lead very dissimilar lives.

Margaret Smith would be quieter than the others and in some ways have less stressful conditions as she is usually fortunate, likes peace and quiet and believes everything will work out fine.

Margaret Johnson would be the best leader, very sociable and popular with friends, as well as capable communicating and organizing people.

Margaret Walters may be clear headed, but quick to judge and sarcastic. This is due to another A coming from the Walters adding to the two already present in Margaret. She will likely be secretive, not reveal much about herself, yet keen to know about everybody else. She will be eager to work, especially hands on with small or fine detailed projects.

Margaret Johnson would most likely prefer living in the city, whereas the other two would be split between both, maybe working by week in the city and escaping on weekends to the country. Margaret 38 (11) is a city girl who likes to be around people. Walters 26 (8) likes the countryside with peace and quiet to relax. Smith 24 (6) loves both the land and peace and harmony.

Each of these three Margaret's would have different mother's maiden names and most likely different birthdays. Some may have middle names, making their characteristics even more diverse.

As another example, take the name Harry. The relevant number for Harry is 34 with 7 being the reduced number. The 7 tells us Harry will be friendly and a good communicator. He will also be reserved, not because he wishes to be so, but because he cannot help it. Whenever anything touches his emotions, he will try to conceal it from people. The deeper the feeling, the more he will hide it. He will also be very determined and persevering.

The H in Harry, especially as it is the first letter of his name, will keep him constantly straining or making an effort to get ahead. The A will make him very clear headed. Double R indicates that a large percentage of his life will be busy, rushing around. The letter Y can bring success from his endeavors.

If his name is Harry Green, the latter name being 31, he will likely have practical sense, caution, and an inclination to save money. If he makes investments, it will likely be after careful thought. If his chart shows he is in the G from Green, it will be a safe or successful investment, especially if the A from Harry enhanced his mental vision when he made the decision.

If on the other hand, his name were Harry Louis, with the Louis being 22, it is very possible he might spend his money freely or be extravagant if the pendulum of 22 swings in a negative direction. He might then have fits of economy and save when positive influences give him better direction. This will be a peculiar phase of character which his friends will be quite unable to comprehend and will likely render him an enigma to himself. If he makes an investment when his events chart shows he is in the letter U, it will almost certainly be a bad decision as the U indicates loss. Positive or negative influences will affect the pendulum of 22, bringing out the best or worst in his character. The 22 is capable of great achievement or capable of great disaster.

Take one more hypothetical comparison, James 12 (3), Brown 27 (9), Smith 24 (6) and Rudolph 40 (4), Sidney 31 (4), Darrad 28 (1).

James Brown Smith would be gentle, sweet tempered, likely to be very reserved enjoying life in the background, have musical interests, a big imagination and not worry too much. Rudolph, on the other hand, with three extrovert names, would be practical but have very little imagination. His temper would likely flare with the slightest provocation. He would never shrink into the background, wanting to take as much of the foreground as he could possible cover. He might be hands on and mechanically minded but would be too contrary and self opinionated ever to rise to genius. He would be a most uncomfortable person to be with, opposing everyone and everything, and altogether an individual to avoid whenever possible.

Before we look at the world of high profile recognized celebrities, I would like to demonstrate by names a very special man I met recently. He has been very instrumental in helping me discover important information to finalize this book. From an early age, he was an outstanding scholar. He became a successful medical doctor and then moved on to homeopathic treatment. He is respected for his expertise worldwide as a homeopathic doctor with intuitive insight. His name is Dr. Tito Palacio, born on the 5th April 1959.

T I T O		R O D O L F O		P A L A C I O		H E N R Y
19/26		**40/32**		**30/42**		**34/20**
1/8		**4/5**		**3/6**		**7/2**

Using the primary reduced numbers first for a quick calculation, we take 1, 4, 3, and 7 with birthday 5. None of these numbers immediately appear to clash like mixing a 4 with a 9 and there is only one potential number showing physical nerves, the 5. This combination does not set off any alarm bells especially as 19, 40, 30 and 34 are not abnormal numbers with problems. Therefore, we can assume very little negative will come from this combination and we can focus on the positive comments.

1 is active and energetic, 4 is open minded, 3 is caring and capable of taking control, 7 makes him a potentially good business man and 5 gives him intelligence with some zest.

Now, take a look at the big picture. One name with nerves can be good. There is another 5 in his undertone. Undertone nerves have less impact and in this case it is a 32, which rarely has nervous problems, instead it makes him very sociable and fast paced. Looking at all the reduced numbers, he has one of each, 1 to 8. This is good, especially as there are no 9's to conflict with his 4. Once again, we can assume the balance is good with no excess nerves and no conflict with 4's and 9's. He only has one pendulum number, the number 4, but as his balance is good we can assume he is getting the best side of that number. He does not have an 11 or a 22. To add one of these numbers would put him on the edge and to add both would put him into nervous overload. This man is very happy with himself and his life. He has complete balance.

The 42 is an *abnormal* number that needs to be given careful consideration even though it is an undertone. As he is not getting any negative influences from his events chart or other names, again he will benefit from the positive side of this number. It will add strength to the primary number 30. He will always have good intentions. A closer look at the personality for 42 will tell you this is quite a remarkable man who walks in the light. I can tell you that every positive comment in 42 is Tito Palacio.

Number 20 can be a good personality but is also marked *abnormal.* Those with number 20 can sometimes lack confidence. As Tito has balance and positive attitude from his primary names, the confidence issue from his undertone 20 is limited to a few seconds of distraction or hesitation.

Taking a few traits from each of the reduced numbers, his profile would read as follows. He is quick, active, energetic and fun to be with. He is very caring and has both a quick brain and an open mind. He is intelligent, artistic, logical and optimistic. He is always striving to get ahead or improve his skills but likes peace and quiet to relax. He has a good business mind and is good communicating. He likes making money but is prepared to work for it. He is good with detail. He can be friendly and talkative. He usually has something good to say and is worth listening to.

Now refer to the full personality definition pages 1 to 64 and read all of the numbers for Tito Palacio. Most of the positive comments reflect this man's personality. This is a perfect example where you read only the positive for every name. The negative will rarely come out because he is balanced and happy.

The second determining factor is his chart. Negative letters or negative letter combinations will upset the balance. When people are not happy, they tend to step out of character and do negative things, out of frustration or boredom.

However, the letters in his names are mostly good. He has a lot of O's, which could make him a little slow in physical movement, but names 19, 32 and his birthday 5 are very active, so again we have balance. There is usually one R somewhere in his chart, which also helps keep him active and busy to also compensate for the O's. The letter I will increase his intuitiveness making him kind and sensitive. The F will be his desire to search and find knowledge, not concealment. When he is in the letter H from Henry, he will be striving more so to get ahead, because it brings him pleasure. There are no brick walls along his path, so he has complete control of his destiny. With a positive attitude, he instinctively opens good doors every day.

Chapter Fourteen

LOOK AT FAMOUS NAMES

My interpretations for names of the people in this chapter, both alive and dead, are related to public knowledge available on the Internet. I have based my comments on information gathered from previously published reports and not from my personal speculation. It is not my intention to defame or slander any of the people named in this chapter. I allow you, the reader, the opportunity to decide if my assessments are accurate, irrelevant or conveniently co-incidental to the truth.

My website shows more names of people currently in the media.

www.namesdoctor.com

I could write several pages for each of the personalities in this chapter. Rather than write volumes about a few names, I will give you more names and focus more on the relevant facts you will recognize from their highly publicized lives.

Where do I start? Not an easy choice for me because each and every name I have researched has been an adventure. Here are a few I hope you enjoy!

Rihanna

Chris Brown

Tyler Perry

Simon Cowell

Tiger Woods

Catherine Zeta Jones

Michael Jackson

Margaret Thatcher

Amy Winehouse

George Best

Paul Gazza Gascoigne

Heath Ledger

Oscar Pistorious

O. J. Simpson

Lindsay Lohan

Charlie Sheen

Various Sex-a-holics

Jimmy Savile

Robyn **Rihanna** Fenty Braithwaite. 20 February 1988.

R O B Y N		R I H A N N A		F E N T Y		B R A I T H W A I T E		20
29/25		38/43		25/20		44/64		20
11/7		11/7		7/2		8/1		2

2004	2005	2006	2007	2008	2009	2010	2011	2012	2013	2014	2015	2016
16	17	18	19	20	21	22	23	24	25	26	27	28
b	y	y	y	y	y	y	y	n	n	n	n	n
i	i	h	h	h	h	h	h	h	h	a	n	n
t	t	y	y	y	y	y	y	y	F	F	F	F
i	i	i	i	i	t	t	h	h	h	h	h	h

With two 11's and two 2's, it is clear that Rihanna has a lot of mental activity with a strong desire to work and get ahead from the three 7's. The Y's in her names came at the right time, opening doors and giving her a clear path to show the world her talent.

Read all of her individual personalities. Her primary numbers are dominant with an influence from each undertone. Rihanna sees the glass half full and strives to fill it. (29) She has a strong personality and is not afraid to speak her mind. (38) Good communicating and networking. (25) A desire for fame, fortune and recognition, (44) with an eye for detail. (20)

Her profile on Wikipedia confirms that in 2004 she moved to the USA (when in the letters B I T I). This combination indicates a very emotional tense time with change of home, career or both. Her career took off in 2005 (Y). Double Y, the next year doubled her success. The single letter H, made her strive to get ahead, but the double H, starting on her 23rd birthday, suggests work and life became stressful. The Y's indicating extreme success ended when she turned 25. However, with such a huge following, she would have to do something very silly to fall out of the limelight. Her chart does indicate 2013/14 will be a stressful year. The F could be people concealing things from her and it is likely she will try to conceal her personal emotions from others. Next year will be better when the H from Rihanna ends. She may use this time to (F) *find* herself a new direction. In 2015, double N indicates double love, maybe a baby? Unfortunately, if Rihanna lets the stress affect her life, the double N can indicate health. With so many 11's and 2's in her names, it could affect the head area producing headaches or insomnia. Rihanna will find it beneficial to channel her excess nerves into productive mental activity when she retires from the stage spotlight.

Rihanna's on-off boyfriend Chris Brown just cannot help being an unpredictable bad boy. My calculations show him as undertone dominant. He has physical nerves twice, from the 59 and his birthday number 5. The number 47 from Maurice gives him mental nerves. The introvert 27 from Brown, conflicts with his extrovert birthday, number 5. The 41 adds more activity whilst at the same time giving him some control of his emotions, though this will probably only show when he is relaxed and in introvert mode from his 27. He may be getting an influence from his nickname Chris, which would be 30/33. However if this is the case, it will not add much control because from age 20 to 29 he is in the letter I which doubles up on the I he already has in his chart for the next few years. His astrological path may bring him success, but is he really happy?

Christopher Maurice **Brown** Hawkins. 5 May 1989.

C H R I S T O P H E R		M A U R I C E		B R O W N		H A W K I N S		5
13/59		34/47		27/27		31/41		5
4/5		7/11		9/9		4/5		5

2008	2009	2010	2011	2012	2013	2014	2015	2016	2017	2018	2019	2020	2021	2022	2023
19	20	21	22	23	24	25	26	27	28	29	30	31	32	33	34
i	i	i	i	i	i	s	s	s	s	s	s	s	s	t	t
r	r	r	r	r	r	r	r	r	i	i	i	i	i	i	i
w	w	w	w	n	n	n	n	B	B	B	B	B	B	B	r
k	i	i	i	i	i	i	i	i	i	n	n	n	n	s	s

The letters in his chart from age 19 show high emotions from the letter I. The letter K is usually positive, but in a combination like this, with the R (too busy) and W (wavering conditions, anxiety, self-doubt), it makes one rash and nervous. Add to this his edgy personality and it is easy to see how he lost control with his girlfriend Rihanna at this time. The letter N for loving conditions started on his birthday in 2012. During this time, he made up with Rihanna and rekindled their relationship, although as I write this page, it appears to be off again. I am sure he is ready to love her, but with so many variables coming into to play, it will not be easy an easy journey.

Tyler Perry Campbell. 13 September 1969

T	Y	L	E	R		P	E	R	R	Y		C	A	M	P	B	E	L	L		13
26/28						37/26						28/44									13
8/1						1/8						1/8									4

1990	1991	1992	1993	1994	1995	1996	1997	1998	1999	2000	2001	2002
21	22	23	24	25	26	27	28	29	30	31	32	33
r	r	r	r	r	T	T	y	y	y	y	y	y
r	r	r	r	r	r	r	r	r	y	y	y	y
e	l	l	l	l	l	l	C	C	C	a	m	m

2003	2004	2005	2006	2007	2008	2009	2010	2011	2012	2013	2014	2015
34	35	36	37	38	39	40	41	42	43	44	45	46
y	l	l	l	e	e	e	e	e	r	r	r	r
y	y	y	P	P	P	P	P	P	P	e	e	e
m	m	p	p	p	p	p	p	p	b	b	e	e

Tyler Perry is best known in the USA for his roles as actor, director, screenplay, playwright, producer and author. In 2011, *Forbes* named him the highest paid man in the entertainment industry. Wikipedia tells how this man came from very difficult beginnings. He legally changed his name at the age of 16 from Emmitt, (his father's name) to Tyler, in a bid to rid himself of any connection to his abusive father.

At the time, I suspect he did not know how much this would change his life. The Y, L and E from Tyler replaced what would have been E, M and I in his chart. Tyler's chart from his 28th birthday went from very good to brilliant. Without the name change, Tyler would have been in double M's from the age 32 to 36. Who knows what mishaps may have come his way?

There is no doubt that Tyler is an exceptionally talented man. When he was 22 he put his life savings into a musical play. It failed, but he persisted and rewrote the musical repeatedly even though lackluster reviews continued. At this time, he was in R, R, and L. The L shows change and advancement, usually with more responsibility, though sometimes at self-sacrifice. The double R's you know are not good. Rushing around, making life confusing, difficult and not always making the right decisions. When he was 26 and 27, the letters changed to T, R and L. This was a time when he could focus and make positive changes. He did!

At age 28 in 1998, he succeeded in retooling the play and restaging it in Atlanta. At this time he was in Y, R and C. Busy, successful and in control. The rest is history. You will see his chart went from strength to strength, paving a clear path allowing him to shine.

If we look at his personality numbers you will see 26 and 28 repeat. The 26 says you may have repressed circumstances early in life. However this is offset with self-confidence. You are energetic. You may not be aware you have the ability to take charge or control, but this will prevail, especially in times of emergency. You are good with your hands especially working with fine detail. Good with study. You are driven and will work hard to achieve your goals. You are a clever speaker, usually calm, good with politics or diplomatic departments. You work well with people and would make a good writer. *No kidding!*

The number 28 says you have a strong personality. You can be very extrovert at times. Hard work usually brings you good results and money. You can show good judgment. You are original and inventive finding solutions. You have a versatile constructive and active mind. You are a natural leader and very capable in business, often heading or running a company. You are artistic and good with design.

The number 37 is a good personality for entertainment and the arts. Personality number 44, like Rihanna, brings fame, fortune and recognition.

Simon Phillip **Cowell** Dalglish. Born 7th October 1959.

S I M O N		P H I L L I P		C O W E L L		D A G L I S H		7
25/29		46/35		25/29		36/45		7
7/11		1/8		7/11		9/9		7

1982	1983	1984	1985	1986	1987	1988	1989	1990	1991	1992	1993	1994	1995	1996	1997
23	24	25	26	27	28	29	30	31	32	33	34	35	36	37	38
n	n	S	i	i	i	i	i	i	i	i	i	m	m	m	m
i	l	l	l	l	l	l	i	i	i	i	i	i	i	i	i
l	l	C	C	C	o	o	o	o	o	o	w	w	w	w	w
i	i	i	i	s	h	h	h	h	h	h	h	h	D	D	D

1998	1999	2000	2001	2002	2003	2004	2005	2006	2007	2008	2009	2010	2011	2012	2013
39	40	41	42	43	44	45	46	47	48	49	50	51	52	53	54
o	o	o	o	o	o	n	n	n	n	n	S	i	i	i	i
p	p	p	p	p	p	p	P	P	P	P	P	P	P	h	h
e	e	e	e	e	l	l	l	l	l	l	C	C	C	o	o
D	a	l	l	l	g	g	g	g	g	g	g	l	l	l	i

Simon does not have a perfect balance of names, but then neither does he have a negative balance. Therefore the lowest form will not come out and the negative definitions in his numbers will only show in a mild sense. He has just the right amount of mental nerves to give him an edge, from the undertones of 29. What he does have is a lot of 7's which make him a work-a-holic. 25 and 46 are very intuitive. 25's make him a great networker but stubborn at times, though usually because he is right. 46, like the 25, are good at making money. The 36 has a nice personality and the 45 is thoughtful and caring. All this goes to prove Mr. Cowell is actually a nice guy!

The number 29 can be a very delicate number, easily swayed in the wrong direction. But as Simon has no names to aggravate the negative side, he gains the positive side of 29. The glass is half full, not half empty and he wants to fill it. The 29 is another name that likes to work hard and make money. Incidentally, tycoon Richard Branson, the Virgin founder, also has the 29 twice and a similar quantity of 7's. If you read all the personality numbers you will see why Branson and Cowell are money making machines. Simon's birthday number 7 is the icing on his cake.

Simon Cowell has not an easy path as some may believe. When he turned 28, the letter H came into his chart. The H represents stress and strain. This can go two ways. Stress as in worry, and strain, as in straining or striving harder to get ahead when you believe it will bring good results.

This H started at the time his business venture folded, so we can assume the O was loss of money causing the stress. The L shows there was self-sacrifice during this two year period and the letter I shows his emotions, which obviously were not in good shape.

I would read his chart as stress for the first 2 years of the letter H and then striving to get ahead for the next 4 years because the double I enhanced his intuitiveness. It's almost like he knew there was a pot of gold waiting for him. He just had to keep going until he found it. The last two years of the H were stressful because the W brought wavering conditions with anxiety and doubt.

The wavering times continued, however the H had gone and the D started when he was 36, which combined with the M indicates *big* changes.

Age 39 and 40 is clearly when things really started to happen. The letter O represents money and usually stability. The letter P represents power and success. The A and E just added more activity and extremes to the O and P.

Age 41 was the big one. The L brought change, advancement and more responsibility to the O P and E.

Age 44 his chart went off the chart. The G added to an incredible combination of positive letters, allowing him total and complete freedom to follow his dreams, which he did! His intuitive business sense and relentless determination came through with a big result.

October 7th 2012 the power letters had gone, but he was striving (H) to make more money (O), using his intuitive ability (I) to advance (L). Is there is no stopping this man?

Tiger Woods Eldrick Tont Woods Punsawad (Tiger).
Born 30 December 1975.

E L D R I C K		T O N T		W O O D S		P U N S A W A D		T I G E R		30
35/46		15/21		22/23		27/45		32/31		30
8/1		6/3		22/5		9/9		5/4		3

1997	1998	1999	2000	2001	2002	2003	2004	2005	2006	2007	2008	2009	2010	2011	2012	2013
22	23	24	25	26	27	28	29	30	31	32	33	34	35	36	37	38
i	i	i	i	i	i	i	i	c	c	c	k	k	E	E	E	E
o	n	n	n	n	n	t	t	T	T	o	o	o	o	o	o	n
W	W	W	W	W	o	o	o	o	o	o	o	o	o	o	o	o
a	d	d	d	d	P	P	P	P	P	P	P	u	u	u	n	n
e	r	r	r	r	r	r	r	r	r	T	T	i	i	i	i	i

I just read how Tiger Woods is back on form and has new love in his life. The last few years have not been good for him according to what you read in the tabloids, so I decided to take a look. Name Reality does not reveal every moment of your life, but usually provides some answers. If you dig deep and look into the personalities first and then analyze how the letters in the chart affect that person, you usually come up with something.

Answers do not always show as strong as in this example for Tiger Woods.

First read the definitions for letters P T O U I and N.

From age 27 Tiger was reaping the benefits of the P adding more power and success. The O was adding more money. Of course he was busy with the R and he was on an emotional high with the letter I. The T which lasts for two years popped up 3 times every year with the P from age 28 which indicates constant change every year. At age 32 he gained a second O which is when things began to slow down a little. The P has a tendency to crash when it comes to an end unless you have good supporting letters. Tiger did not have good supporting letters, he went into the U which is very negative and indicates loss. When he was 35 he was in double O for slow, U for loss and I for his emotions, which undoubtedly were shot. All of this was then exaggerated by the E to compound and make everything worse. No wonder his personal life and his game fell apart.

Tiger's birthday is the 30th December. On the first week of 2013, the U had gone and N for love came back into his life. By the middle of 2013, he was back.

If you read all of his personality numbers you can see why he is so great and yet sometimes a rogue. Immediately I see 22 conflicting with 27 which bring out a lot of the negative in his names and in some cases the lowest form. The tabloids branded him a sex-a-holic which is not true. The lowest form of 30 is infidelity, meaning very sexually active, of which he is guilty. The good sided nature of 30 is it adds some control to his volatile 22 and 27.

On his 38th birthday at the end of 2013 his chart loses an O and gains an N. Life will speed up again in 2014 and he will get double love. The big question is will he be an infidel bad boy again, or will the new N be another little Tiger?

Catherine Zeta Jones.

When I read in the news that Catherine was diagnosed with bipolar II disorder, I thought, *here is a challenge for me*. The challenge was short lived. When I calculated her names, immediately I saw the numbers 47, 16/20 and the undertone 29 from Fair, her mother's maiden name. When Catherine married Michael Douglas, she got another shot of mental nerves with the undertone 38 from Douglas. Zeta can be a lovely name, but not with Catherine, Fair and Douglas. This amount of names with mental nervous energy puts Catherine on a knife edge and very susceptible to circumstances and the letters in her chart.

Catherine Zeta Jones Fair. Born 25 Sept 1969.

C A T H E R I N E		Z E T A		J O N E S		F A I R		25
47/52		16/20		18/27		25/29		25
11/7		7/2		9/9		7/11		7

1969	1970	1971	1972	1973	1974	1975	1976	1977	1978	1979	1980	1981	1982	1983
0	1	2	3	4	5	6	7	8	9	10	11	12	13	14
C	C	C	a	t	t	h	h	h	h	h	h	h	h	e
Z	Z	Z	Z	Z	Z	Z	Z	e	e	e	e	e	t	t
j	o	o	o	o	o	o	n	n	n	n	n	e	e	e
F	F	F	F	F	F	a	i	i	i	i	i	i	i	i

1984	1985	1986	1987	1988	1989	1990	1991	1992	1993	1994	1995	1996	1997	1998	1999	2000
15	16	17	18	19	20	21	22	23	24	25	26	27	28	29	30	31
e	e	e	e	r	r	r	r	r	r	r	r	r	i	i	i	i
a	Z	Z	Z	Z	Z	Z	Z	Z	e	e	e	e	e	t	t	a
e	e	s	J	o	o	o	o	o	o	n	n	n	n	n	e	e
i	r	r	r	r	r	r	r	r	r	F	F	F	F	F	F	a

2000	2001	2002	2003	2004	2005	2006	2007	2008	2009	2010	2011	2012	2013	2014	2015
31	32	33	34	35	36	37	38	39	40	41	42	43	44	45	46
i	i	i	i	i	i	n	n	n	n	n	e	e	e	e	e
a	Z	Z	Z	Z	Z	Z	Z	Z	e	e	e	e	e	t	t
e	e	e	e	s	J	o	o	o	o	o	o	n	n	n	n
a	i	i	i	i	i	i	i	i	i	r	r	r	r	r	r
o	o	o	o	u	u	u	g	g	g	g	g	g	g	l	l

When I ran the events chart all I could see were R's, I's and E's. It would appear the only time Catherine has any peace, is when she is very busy with work, burning up the excess energy, or when the negative letters are not in her chart. I suspect life was uneasy from age 8, but more so at age 12. H E E I. At age 13 and 14 the letter T can indicate change, but I fear this may have affected her head, worsening conditions. I have seen a similar chart where this combination produced a period of anorexia until the T finished. On Catherine's 16th birthday, she received the letter R from Fair, together with double E and Z. I do not suspect the Z added much control until she was 18. Despite the letters going into double R's, the letter O together with the Z would add some stability as long as she kept busy and burned up that energy. Age 24, I suspect was not a good year emotionally. Age 25 appears better. I think the N indicated how much she loved her work. However the F suggests that she was concealing some of her anxiety. The letter T for change, was about to come back in 1998 when she was 29. At this time, she was still in the letter N and met Michael Douglas. Love is a wonderful cure. This was also the time when her career on the big screen took off with the movie Zorro followed by Entrapment the following year. The R's were gone and the Z came back adding control and strong health.

Unfortunately, the R came back with an E in 2010 on her 41st birthday. Then in 2011 another E added to the equation. Age 43 and 44 the chart shows E E N R G. This is a very nervous combination of letters for somebody with names like Catherine. At age 45 and 46 one of the E's is replaced with a T and the G is replaced with an L. This combination of letters can go in one of two directions. The T could mean change, or it could indicate the head. The N can bring love, strong love with the T, or add nerves and indicate sensitive health. The L like the T can bring change for the better and the L can strengthen health. However, it can come with some self-sacrifice. The R and the E are not a good combination with Catherine's names. These two letters can make or break this two year period. If Catherine can find ways to channel her excess mental energy and at the same time, find natural ways to relax and sleep, these two years can be very productive. Awareness is the key. Catherine, I hope you read this book.

Playing with names for Catherine, I came up with some options.

Cattylyn C. Zytaa Jones G. Douglas. Born 25th September 1969

<table>
<tr><td>C</td><td>A</td><td>T</td><td>T</td><td>Y</td><td>L</td><td>Y</td><td>N</td><td></td><td>C</td><td></td><td>Z</td><td>Y</td><td>T</td><td>A</td><td>A</td><td></td><td>J</td><td>O</td><td>N</td><td>E</td><td>S</td><td></td><td>G</td><td></td><td>D</td><td>O</td><td>U</td><td>G</td><td>L</td><td>A</td><td>S</td><td></td><td>25</td></tr>
<tr><td colspan="8">30/42</td><td></td><td>3/6</td><td></td><td colspan="5">19/26</td><td></td><td colspan="5">18/27</td><td></td><td>7/2</td><td></td><td colspan="7">25/38</td><td></td><td>25</td></tr>
</table>

2013	2014	2015	2016	2017	2018	2019	2020	2021	2022	2023	2024	2025	2026	2027	2028
44	45	46	47	48	49	50	51	52	53	54	55	56	57	58	59
y	l	l	l	y	y	y	y	y	y	y	n	n	n	n	n
C	C	C	C	C	C	C	C	C	C	C	C	C	C	C	C
Z	Z	y	y	y	y	y	y	y	t	t	a	a	Z	Z	Z
n	n	n	n	e	e	e	e	e	s	J	o	o	o	o	o
G	G	G	G	G	G	G	G	G	G	G	G	G	G	G	G
g	l	l	l	a	s	D	D	D	D	o	o	o	o	o	o

Or, maybe change Catherine to Kathyryn which is 41/40 and change Zeta to simply Z. The Z works well for Jay-Z!

Michael Jackson Michael Joseph Jackson Scruse. Born 29 August 1958

M I C H A E L		J O S E P H		J A C K S O N		S C R U S E		29
33/39		28/26		19/44		22/41		29
6/3		1/8		1/8		22/5		11

1992	1993	1994	1995	1996	1997	1998	1999	2000	2001	2002	2003	2004	2005	2006	2007	2008
34	35	36	37	38	39	40	41	42	43	44	45	46	47	48	49	50
M	M	M	i	i	i	i	i	i	i	i	i	c	c	c	h	h
o	s	e	e	e	e	e	p	p	p	p	p	p	p	h	h	h
n	n	n	n	J	a	c	c	c	k	k	s	o	o	o	o	o
r	u	u	u	s	e	e	e	e	e	S	c	c	c	r	r	r

Michael Jackson, the King of Pop, had a very complicated life. Some parts are well documented. His life chart would be difficult to fully analyze without all the facts. A Name Reality chart is not just about financial success, it is also very much about personal feelings and emotions. Michael was very secretive and sensitive, so it is not easy to assume what was going on in this man's mind. His life chart is a roller coaster with downs where you would expect ups and vice versa.

The sexual abuse allegations started in 1993. Regardless if he did or didn't, the humiliation hurt Michael in so many ways, indicated by the letters. M indicates change. S sharpens all the letters of that year. N indicates love, but lost like everything else from the U. The following year was very similar and the next was probably worse when the letter I signified his emotions. His death, when he was only 50 shows he was extremely stressed with financial problems. H H O R.

His name personality numbers are a very diverse combination. If you read them one by one and compare them with what is known about his life, you will see he was a very complicated yet brilliant man.

Margaret Thatcher 1925–2013. UK Prime Minister 1979–1990.

I have included Margaret Thatcher because she is a perfect example how excess work can burn up excess nerves from your names and your events chart.

Margaret Hilda Roberts Stephenson Thatcher. Born 13th October 1925

M A R G A R E T		H I L D A		R O B E R T S		S T E P H E N S O N		T H A T C H E R		13
38/52		25/29		34/47		45/45		38/43		13
11/7		7/11		7/11		9/9		11/7		4

1974	1975	1976	1977	1978	1979	1980	1981	1982	1983	1984	1985	1986	1987	1988	1989	1990
49	50	51	52	53	54	55	56	57	58	59	60	61	62	63	64	65
r	r	r	g	g	g	g	g	g	g	a	r	r	r	r	r	r
a	H	H	H	H	H	H	H	H	i	i	i	i	i	i	i	i
b	b	e	e	e	e	e	r	r	r	r	r	r	r	r	r	t
e	e	e	e	p	p	p	p	p	p	p	h	h	h	h	h	h
t	t	c	c	c	h	h	h	h	h	h	h	h	e	e	e	e

1997	1998	1999	2000	2001	2002	2003	2004	2005	2006	2007	2008	2009	2010	2011	2012
72	73	74	75	76	77	78	79	80	81	82	83	84	85	86	87
e	e	t	t	M	M	M	M	a	r	r	r	r	r	r	r
d	d	a	H	H	H	H	H	H	H	H	i	i	i	i	i
R	R	R	R	R	o	o	o	o	o	o	b	b	e	e	e
e	n	n	n	n	n	s	o	o	o	o	o	o	n	n	n
r	r	r	r	T	T	h	h	h	h	h	h	h	h	a	t

Maggie was always a work-a-holic. The long hours she put in at 10 Downing Street as England's only woman Prime Minister for three terms are well known. Her names have two primary mental nerves and two undertone mental nerves. Her events chart is full of the letters H R I and E, enough to put the average woman into an early grave. But Maggie was not average. You will see that despite the excess mental nerves, she has three *good for business* number 7's. The 38, 45 and 47 are also very business orientated names. If you were around in England during her term as PM, or know about her life, please do read her numbers. You will understand why she had the natural ability to lead a country.

Looking at her chart, in 1953 she was in R H R N R, the first year of the letter N, appropriate as she gave birth to her twins. 1975 Maggie was in the first year of the letter T from R H B E T, the T signifying change. She beat Edward Heath as the leader for the conservative party. In 1979 she was in her first year of the letter P, together with G H E H, this was the year she came to power. In 1983 she was in G I R P H when she won the re-election. Despite winning another election, the tides turned on her popularity and the positive letters were long gone from her chart. On her 65th birthday she went into stressful letters R I T H E. The T for change, that she had experienced in 1979, when she won the election, would now be a T for change in the opposite direction. She was forced to step down as Prime Minister.

Maggie was an active figure for another 10 years. When she was 76 and 77 the T came back again, this time bringing poor health. When she was 77 and in the last year of the letter N for love, her beloved husband Dennis passed away. Soon after, she was diagnosed with dementia, which is not surprising considering her age and names. She still had the excess mental energy, but with no mental work producing means for escape. This was further exaggerated by a stressful events chart. She died in the first year of yet another letter T, when she was 87. Comfortingly, she was in the peak of the letter N, bringing love to her final days.

Whether you liked her or disliked her, you have to admit, she was one hell of a woman.

Amy Jade **Winehouse** Seaton + Civil 2007. Born 14 September 1983.

A M Y		J A D E		W I N E H O U S E		S E A T O N		C I V I L		14
12/15		11/25		47/43		20/34		28/35		14
3/6		11/7		11/7		2/7		1/8		5

1997	1998	1999	2000	2001	2002	2003	2004	2005	2006	2007	2008	2009	2010
14	15	16	17	18	19	20	21	22	23	24	25	26	27
m	m	m	y	y	y	y	y	y	y	A	m	m	m
d	d	d	e	e	e	e	e	J	a	d	d	d	d
n	n	n	n	n	e	e	e	e	e	h	h	h	h
o	n	n	n	n	n	S	e	e	e	e	e	a	t
										i	l	l	l

Amy Winehouse in some ways reminds me of Margaret Thatcher. Amy had two mental nerves in her primary and physical nerves from her birthday. Amy was another woman with great talent, drive and determination. Unfortunately, she was in the entertainment business, where after hours shop time is party-party and party. Shop talk would likely have been, have another shot or do another line, a far cry from Maggie and her political debates with a cup of tea.

I cannot confirm if Amy legally used her married name of Civil. However, I suspect she did and it did add fuel to her fire. The 28 is a very active number which together with the volatile 11 and unpredictable 14 would explain her outbursts. From information on Wikipedia and other internet websites, it would appear her decline started on her 24th birthday. The letters E with Y for extreme success ended and the letters E and H for extreme stress started. Name Reality shows why Russell Brand was able to overcome his addiction problems whilst Amy could not. Copies of this book have been sent to Mitch Winehouse at the Amy Winehouse Foundation and Focus 12, sponsored by Russell Brand.

Sadly, she passed away when only 27 years old due to excessive alcohol consumption. Gladly, she left behind her music which will entertain many for generations to come. R.I.P Amy.

George Best Withers. Born 22 May 1946.

G E O R G E		B E S T		W I T H E R S		22
39/24		10/26		39/42		22
3/6		1/8		3/6		22

George Best was a 1960's UK soccer icon. Even the great Pele conceded George was one of the best players of his time. Unfortunately, he drank himself to death, dying in 2005 at the age of 59 from liver related complications. Why?

His chart is relatively uneventful. The only positive letters he had are the two G's in George which did not coincide at the time when he peaked as a player for Manchester United. He does have the letter E in every name and they frequently doubled up or coincided with the letter R which is not a good combination. The last three years of his life, he was not in particularly good letters, but neither were they life threating.

1958	1959	1960	1961	1962	1963	1964	1965	1966	1967	1968	1969	1970	1971	1972	1973
12	13	14	15	16	17	18	19	20	21	22	23	24	25	26	27
o	o	o	o	o	o	r	r	r	r	r	r	r	r	r	g
e	e	e	e	e	s	t	t	B	B	e	e	e	e	e	s
i	i	t	t	h	h	h	h	h	h	h	h	e	e	e	e

1974	1975	1976	1977	1978	1979	1980	1981	1982	1983	1984	1985	1986	1987	1988	1989
28	29	30	31	32	33	34	35	36	37	38	39	40	41	42	43
g	g	g	g	g	g	e	e	e	e	e	G	G	G	G	G
t	t	B	B	e	e	e	e	e	s	t	t	B	B	e	e
e	r	r	r	r	r	r	r	r	r	s	W	W	W	W	W

1990	1991	1992	1993	1994	1995	1996	1997	1998	1999	2000	2001	2002	2003	2004	2005
44	45	46	47	48	49	50	51	52	53	54	55	56	57	58	59
G	G	e	e	e	e	e	o	o	o	o	o	o	r	r	r
e	e	e	s	t	t	B	B	e	e	e	e	e	s	t	t
i	i	i	i	i	i	i	i	i	t	t	h	h	h	h	h

His personality numbers helped with his rise to fame, but at the same time were the root of his problems. The letter combinations in his chart would aggravate the negative side of his character.

The number 39 can be associated to many great people. In a balanced combination of names, 39 can rise to a high position. The actor George Clooney has done well with his name. Unfortunately 39, whilst having the ability to rise, can fall just as fast. George Best has the 39 repeat in his mother's maiden name of Withers. The undertone with this name is 42. Not a good combination in a less than perfect balance of names. The name Best is a very active 10, which though good for sport was not good for the 39 and 42. The whole combination is then seriously affected by the pendulum birthday number 22. Capable of great achievement or great disaster and sometimes both!

The number 39 with 22 is known for producing very high sex drive. This was true of George. The 39 is capable of murder. There is no doubt that George knew exactly what he was doing to his body with excessive alcohol. So, it would not be unreasonable to say he killed himself. Incidentally, George's mother Ann 11/16 Withers 39/42, died of alcohol related problems at the age of 55.

This leads me to another British soccer great, Paul Gascoigne, known as Gazza.

Paul is now 46 years old with a history of alcohol problems and domestic violence. Many refer to him as another George Best. Paul was a brilliant player and still is a total disaster.

My calculations put him as undertone dominant. Like George, he has the 22, in his case as his dominant number from the name Paul. The complimenting number of 14, although a brilliant extrovert number, it does have excess physical nerves and makes him unpredictable, especially as his birthday is a conflicting introvert 27. The 46, like George's 10, reduces to a 1, though not as strong. However 46's do tend to have a roller coaster life. The 44 is where he gets his fame and recognition. His drunken outbursts come from the volatile 16 with additional violence thrown in for good measure from his 31. The worst year of his chart is age 59, coincidentally the same age when George Best departed.

So, Mr. Gascoigne, a copy of this book is being delivered to Elite Welfare Management. Read it and give me a call if you want to change your name.

Paul John **Gascoigne** Harold. Born 27 May 1967.

P A U L		J O H N		G A S C O I G N E		H A R O L D		27
14/22		20/16		44/46		31/32		27
5/22		2/7		8/1		4/5		9

2001	2002	2003	2004	2005	2006	2007	2008	2009	2010	2011	2012	2013	2014	2015	2016
34	35	36	37	38	39	40	41	42	43	44	45	46	47	48	49
u	u	u	u	l	l	l	l	l	l	P	P	a	a	a	a
J	J	J	J	J	J	o	o	o	h	n	n	n	n	J	J
i	i	g	g	n	n	n	n	e	e	e	e	G	G	a	a
a	a	a	a	a	a	a	r	r	r	r	r	r	r	r	r

2017	2018	2019	2020	2021	2022	2023	2024	2025	2026	2027	2028	2029	2030	2031	2032
50	**51**	**52**	**53**	**54**	**55**	**56**	**57**	**58**	**59**	**60**	**61**	**62**	**63**	**64**	**65**
a	a	a	a	u	u	u	u	u	u	l	l	l	l	l	l
J	J	J	J	J	J	o	o	o	h	n	n	n	n	J	J
a	a	a	a	a	a	s	s	s	s	s	s	s	s	c	c
o	o	o	l	l	l	l	l	l	d	d	d	d	d	H	a

Heath Andrew **Ledger** Ramshaw. Born 4 April 1979.

H	E	A	T	H		A	N	D	R	E	W		L	E	D	G	E	R		R	A	M	S	H	A	W		4
24/21						29/34							33/30							29/43								4
6/3						11/7							6/3							11/7								4

1993	1994	1995	1996	1997	1998	1999	2000	2001	2002	2003	2004	2005	2006	2007	2008
14	15	16	17	18	19	20	21	22	23	24	25	26	27	28	29
t	t	h	h	h	h	h	h	h	h	H	H	H	H	H	H
r	r	r	r	r	e	e	e	e	e	w	w	w	w	w	A
g	g	g	g	g	e	e	e	e	e	r	r	r	r	r	r
s	h	h	h	h	h	h	h	h	a	w	w	w	w	w	R

So sad, a lovely man with insecurity problems created by the number 29 repeating and the pendulum birthday number 4. The letters in his chart show what a dreadful time he was personally experiencing leading up to his drug overdose death when only 28 years old. R.I.P Heath.

Oscar Leonard Carl **Pistorious**. Born 22 November 1986.

O S C A R		L E O N A R D		C A R L		P I S T O R I O U S		22
20/34		33/39		16/29		53/64		22
2/7		6/3		7/11		8/1		22

1999	2000	2001	2002	2003	2004	2005	2006	2007	2008	2009	2010	2011	2012	2013	2014
13	14	15	16	17	18	19	20	21	22	23	24	25	26	27	28
r	r	r	r	r	r	r	O	O	O	O	O	O	s	c	c
o	n	n	n	n	n	a	r	r	r	r	r	r	r	r	r
l	l	l	C	C	C	a	r	r	r	r	r	r	r	r	r
i	i	i	s	t	t	o	o	o	o	o	o	r	r	r	r

They call him Blade Runner, the fastest man on no legs. South African double amputee Olympic gold medal winner runs on carbon fiber prosthetics.

In February 2013 he was charged with the murder of his girlfriend Reeva Steenkamp whom he allegedly shot at his home. He was 26 years old at the time.

There is no excuse for taking another person's life. However, to me it is very clear. He was a time bomb about to explode. 16/29 is not a good start, double mental nerves. Add his birthday 22, excess mental nerves with the pendulum. Leonard has 39, capable of murder with a nasty violent temper. The letters in his chart at the time of the alleged murder were S R R R. Quite simply, a Molotov cocktail!

I have been unable to find his mother's maiden name to complete the chart, but it's clear to see that it will make little difference. R.I.P Reeva.

O J Simpson. Orenthal James Simpson Durden. O J Born 9 July 1947.

O	R	E	N	T	H	A	L		J	A	M	E	S		S	I	M	P	S	O	N		D	U	R	D	E	N		O		J		9
39/42									12/33						33/39								30/33							6/3		1/8		9

The number 39 is kind, loving and capable of great achievement when positive. However with negative influences, it can be one of the worst numbers, especially when combined with 42. Please read numbers 39 and 42, together with 1 and 9.

Did he do it?

With 39 and 42, it is very difficult to stay out of trouble, especially when combined with other numbers that add friction. In his case the friction came from the initial J which is a 1 with *too much energy.* The 1 will conflict with his introvert birthday of 9, making him a sweetheart one minute (12) and a disaster the next (39/42). O J was in letters R A S R when Nicole Simpson and Ron Goldman were murdered. R.I.P.

39/42 is not a good combination.

Unless complimented with a beautiful balance of names, 39 with 42 will struggle at best. The level of trouble this combination can bring its owner depends upon their other names and letters in their events chart.

George Best suffered with 39/42 as does Charlie Sheen, Britney Spears, Cameron *Morrell* Douglas, the troubled incarcerated son of Michael Douglas. I am sure the world has many more.

Lindsay Lohan. Lindsay Dee Lohan Sullivan. Born 2 July 1986

L	I	N	D	S	A	Y		D	E	E		L	O	H	A	N		S	U	L	L	I	V	A	N		2
30/42								14/13				23/22						29/52									2
3/6								5/4				5/22						11/7									2

Sometimes she uses names Morgan and Jade.

M	O	R	G	A	N		J	A	D	E	
32/31							11/25				
5/4							11/7				

2003	2004	2005	2006	2007	2008	2009	2010	2011	2012	2013	2014	2015	2016	2017	2018
17	18	19	20	21	22	23	24	25	26	27	28	29	30	31	32
d	d	d	d	s	a	y	y	y	y	y	y	y	L	L	L
D	e	e	e	e	e	e	e	e	e	e	D	D	D	D	e
a	n	n	n	n	n	L	L	L	o	o	o	o	o	o	h
i	i	v	v	v	v	a	n	n	n	n	n	S	u	u	u

Add Morgan and Jade

2003	2004	2005	2006	2007	2008	2009	2010	2011	2012	2013	2014	2015	2016	2017	2018
17	18	19	20	21	22	23	24	25	26	27	28	29	30	31	32
d	d	d	d	s	a	y	y	y	y	y	y	y	L	L	L
D	e	e	e	e	e	e	e	e	e	e	D	D	D	D	e
a	n	n	n	n	n	L	L	L	o	o	o	o	o	o	h
i	i	v	v	v	v	a	n	n	n	n	n	S	u	u	u
r	r	g	g	g	g	g	g	g	a	n	n	n	n	n	M
e	e	e	e	e	J	a	d	d	d	d	e	e	e	e	e

Very little explanation required with Lindsay. Her life is publicized worldwide.

This talented, smart woman seems unable to help herself. She falls in dung yet comes out smelling of roses. I think her luck will run out when she turns 32.

Again, we see excess nerves. She has 14, 23 and 29 in her primary and 22 in her undertone. This combination shows in her pendulum 42. When positive, she walks in the light. When negative, her life can be a struggle, desperately trying to get ahead or to be a good person. Negative balance from other names and negative events can at best create a difficult life or at worst an immoral and destructive or self-destructive life.

I cannot confirm if Lindsay is picking up any vibration from Morgan or Jade. If she is then 32 is the sociable party person and 11 is so capable but with nervous outbursts. If you read all of the numbers for Lindsay, you can see the definitions relate to her personality and her life. Lindsay, please let me change your name!

Charlie Sheen Carlos Irwin Estevez Templeton. Born 3 September 1965.

C H A R L I E	S H E E N	C A R L O S	I R W I N	E S T E V E Z	T E M P L E T O N	3
38/43	24/21	23/40	37/35	30/33	39/42	3
11/7	6/3	5/4	1/8	3/6	3/6	3

2000	2001	2002	2003	2004	2005	2006	2007	2008	2009	2010	2011	2012	2013	2014	2015
35	36	37	38	39	40	41	42	43	44	45	46	47	48	49	50
e	e	e	C	C	C	h	h	h	h	h	h	h	h	a	r
e	e	e	e	e	e	e	e	n	n	n	n	n	S	h	h
r	l	l	l	o	o	o	o	o	o	s	C	C	C	a	r
n	n	I	I	I	I	I	I	I	I	I	r	r	r	r	r
s	t	t	e	e	e	e	e	v	v	v	v	e	e	e	e
n	n	n	n	T	T	e	e	e	e	e	m	m	m	m	p

The infamous bad boy, Charlie Sheen! There is not a lot I can say that hasn't already been said. Quite frankly, it would not really matter what letters were in his chart, he will always self-destruct with his combination of personality numbers.

A name change would be relatively simple you would think?

Remove the Carlos 23/40 and the Templeton 39/42, his mother's maiden name. Voila! Charlie Irwin Estevez Sheen. Maybe throw in an initial G for good measure. The personality numbers are great, but unfortunately, the chart still doesn't flow. Too many E's, R's, I's, W and H.

Name change is rarely simple.

Sex-a-holics

People with high mental activity from a pendulum 22 or 11, if mixed with the very loving and caring 12, 19 or 39, can be very sexually active. Obviously this sexual activity can become a serious problem if other numbers aggravate the trait in a negative direction. For example, some numbers that reduce to 1's and 5's will add physical activity. Some 4's can add aggression. Some 9's will make the owner switch from extroverted to introverted. Letters within the names, especially vowels, will exaggerate or tone down tendencies. The same applies to ones chart. Therefore, some years the person can be more or less sexually active.

Actor Michael Douglas has 22 from his middle name Kirk, 19 from his mother's maiden name Dill and 39 fortunately in the undertone of Michael. His numbers tell me that he has a strong appetite for sex, but not in a negative or aggressive way, partly because the 39 is in his undertone and not in his primary.

Michael 33/39. Kirk 22/32. Douglas 25/38. Dill 19/26. Born 25 September 1944.

Other names the media report as sexually active are; David Duchovny who has 22 from David and 39 in the undertone from his mother's maiden name Miller. Tom Sizemore has Tom 12 and Sizemore 22. Charlie Sheen, has 11 and 39. Maybe these guys should meet up with self-confessed sex-a-holic porn star Kendra Jade Rossi who has 11 from Jade and 19 as her birthday. Or maybe Penny 11, Flame 19, born on the 22nd. Pick any name, they are all the same.

The British media have recently exploited Operation Yewtree, an investigation by the police evolving around the deceased TV personality Jimmy Savile. Evidence shows how this man spent his life using his status to lure young children. He has been branded a predator on an unprecedented scale.

Jimmy James Wilson Vincent **Savile** Kelly. Born 31st October 1926.

J I M M Y		J A M E S		W I L S O N		V I N C E N T		S A V I L E		K E L L Y		31
25/29		12/33		29/34		33/39		23/40		20/25		31
7/11		3/6		11/7		6/3		5/4		2/7		4

Jimmy Savile, undertone dominant by my calculations, is a perfect example where no one name created his problems. The overall *combination* of *all his names* was the problem. Start with two 29 pendulums added with physical nerves from the 23. Combine this with the introvert number 33 that repeats twice and does not balance well with the extrovert numbers 40 and 31. Now add no less than three numbers that normally are kind and loving, but can flip in a sexual direction when negative. Especially the number 39, which in his case was dominant, then add numbers 12 and 20. The 39 has three levels of lowest form; Very sexually active, capable of rape and third, capable of rape and murder with no discretion for age or sex. The number 12 has strong sexual desires. The number 20 reads; you can be thoughtful kind and gentle. Weakness in character can lead to bad choices. Your intentions are always good, even if the result is not always positive. The health warning for number 20 indicates brain or head problems. His events chart is dominated with letters E I S V and W. If you read all of his personality numbers and his profile on Wikipedia, it is not difficult to see his numbers confirm the sad horrific story.

1960	1961	1962	1963	1964	1965	1966	1967	1968	1969	1970	1971	1972	1973	1974	1975
34	35	36	37	38	39	40	41	42	43	44	45	46	47	48	49
J	J	J	J	J	J	J	a	a	a	a	a	a	a	a	m
W	W	W	W	i	i	i	i	i	i	i	i	i	l	l	l
t	t	t	t	t	V	V	V	V	V	i	i	i	i	i	i
l	l	e	e	e	e	S	S	S	S	S	S	S	S	a	a
e	e	l	l	l	l	l	l	l	l	l	l	l	l	y	y
J	J	J	i	i	i	i	i	i	i	i	i	m	m	m	m

1976	1977	1978	1979	1980	1981	1982	1983	1984	1985	1986	1987	1988	1989	1990	1991
50	51	52	53	54	55	56	57	58	59	60	61	62	63	64	65
m	m	m	m	e	e	e	e	s	s	s	s	s	s	s	s
l	l	l	s	s	s	s	s	s	s	s	o	o	o	n	n
i	i	i	n	n	n	n	c	c	c	c	c	c	e	e	e
a	a	a	a	a	a	v	v	v	v	v	i	i	i	i	i
K	K	K	K	K	K	K	e	e	e	e	l	l	l	l	l
m	m	m	m	m	m	y	y	J	J	J	J	J	J	J	J

Chapter Fifteen

CREATE CHANGE OR MODIFY A NAME

For some people, changing their name is a major step while others find it easy as putting on a new jacket. Some like to retain as much of their original name as possible and some want to start over to make a fresh start. This chapter explains simple techniques to create change or to modify your name.

When creating or changing a name, there is no fixed order of what to do first. You want positive letters, but more important, you need to avoid negative letter combinations. You must have names that balance by number. Do not forget the undertones as they are important. You also need a good balance of vowels. You must study your potential events chart to make sure you do not give yourself problems in the future. The Excel program that is available on my website, makes playing with names and numbers fast, accurate and easy.

Regulations to change your name vary from one country to another. Information can usually be found via the Internet relating to your country of birth and location. England is a country where you can change your name with very few restrictions and as often as you please. The paperwork is simple and the whole process costs no more than a replacement passport and driver's license. As long as your name change is for genuine personal reasons to a name that is not offensive and you are not trying to evade the law, the passport office will grant your wish. The passport office in the UK also happens to be the general register office for all civil name registration records. All you need to supply them with is a one page document, known as a Deed Poll. I have prepared these for many of my clients.

Most states in the USA require you to appear in person at your local court. A lawyer is not usually required. The judge will decide if your request is valid and give you permission to change your documents. Court fees and regulations vary from one state to another but are usually three to five hundred dollars.

In Colombia, South America, you can only change your name one time, unless you make a special request at the Supreme Court to change a second time.

You go to a notary who will make a legal name change document for a small fee. You take or send this document to the registration office in the city where you were born and they amend your birth certificate. From there, you use the given papers to change everything you need.

Some countries do not allow you to change your name at all, which in my opinion, is ridiculous and goes against your civil rights. Maybe when this book shows the world just how important names are, changes will be made in those countries.

If you have managed to digest most of the information from the previous chapters, you will know that balance is the key and positive letters are the icing on the cake. It is easy once you get your mind around this system, to create a new name or figure out how to fix a problem. Sometimes, removing one name or changing the way you spell a name can alter the dynamics for the better. Staying away from abnormal personality numbers, too many names with excess nerves and negative letter combinations, is all part of the formula.

The name Ann can be a volatile 11, or Anne, a risky 16. They can be changed to Anna, a very caring and gentle 12 or Ana, a good for business 7. The name Ami is 14. A great number but it has excess physical nerves. If more nerves are coming from the birthday or other names, you can consider changing Ami to Amy, which again is a caring and gentle 12 and the Y brings 7 years of success. It is a process of trial and error. However, sometimes no matter how much you play around with the letters and numbers, nothing comes together. When this happens, you may need to start over with a completely new name.

A clever method that Laurence Payg in England has developed and used is adding initials. The letter G as an initial is the favorite because it brings gains into every year of your life. The letter G represents 7 with 2 as an undertone. Together, they make an incredibly good combination.

Laurence also uses the letter C as an initial, which relates to 3 with 6 as the undertone. The 3 is caring, the C adds control and aids health. The 6 brings out creative or artistic ability with a tranquil personality.

One of his favorite combinations is to use three initials, C, N and G. It is very important each letter is separated on your documentation or CNG will be interpreted as one name and become personality number 15. The C. N and G. can work very well in most cases, but not all. The N, although it is a powerful letter bringing loving conditions, represents the number 5. The number 5 has many good traits but does have excess physical nerves. If your birthday or other names have more physical or mental nerves, you will know from reading this book that too many nervous names can put you into overload with less than favorable reactions.

The letter Y can also be used as an initial as it has the same numerical value as the G, 7, and is related to the intuitive 25. Other initials are possible, but as always, great care must be used to maintain balance. The P is also a 7. The P brings power and success but has a tendency towards extravagance and fritting away what you worked so hard for. The P also relates to the abnormal number 16, which is known for bankruptcy and stress affecting the brain. So it is best not to use P as an individual initial. The letter K is a vivifying force but is related to the number 11, adding nerves. Careful calculation and study must be made if you ever consider using these letters as initials only.

I have friends who retained their first and last names and then added C. N. G. as middle initials with excellent results. Mathematically, this configuration would give you five names, with the middle three being very positive letters active each and every year of your life.

Taylor C. N. G. Smith

T	A	Y	L	O	R		C		N		G		S	M	I	T	H
28/35							3/6		5/4		7/2		24/30				
1/8							3/6		5/4		7/2		6/3				

The birthday for Taylor Smith will be the deciding factor. A birthday on the first would add more activity to the 28, which is also a 1. Therefore, the 28 should be used with caution or avoided if you are looking for a quiet relaxed life. If his birthday were the 5th then I would simply remove the initial N to prevent a double up on the physical nerves. The Smith has one I which will bring some emotions into this man's life, but it would be better if the first or last name were modified to have a letter N within the spelling to help bring more love. The name Antonio is 34. It would work well for leadership, communication, business and love. It has two N's. Everybody can benefit from love and loving conditions.

Here is an example of what the chart would look like for Taylor C. N. G. Smith.

0	1	2	3	4	5	6	7	8	9	10	11	12	13	14	15	16	17	18
T	T	a	y	y	y	y	y	y	y	l	l	l	o	o	o	o	o	o
C	C	C	C	C	C	C	C	C	C	C	C	C	C	C	C	C	C	C
N	N	N	N	N	N	N	N	N	N	N	N	N	N	N	N	N	N	N
G	G	G	G	G	G	G	G	G	G	G	G	G	G	G	G	G	G	G
S	m	m	m	m	i	i	i	i	i	i	i	i	i	t	t	h	h	h

19	20	21	22	23	24	25	26	27	28	29	30	31	32	33	34	35	36	37
r	r	r	r	r	r	r	r	r	T	T	a	y	y	y	y	y	y	y
C	C	C	C	C	C	C	C	C	C	C	C	C	C	C	C	C	C	C
N	N	N	N	N	N	N	N	N	N	N	N	N	N	N	N	N	N	N
G	G	G	G	G	G	G	G	G	G	G	G	G	G	G	G	G	G	G
h	h	h	h	h	S	m	m	m	m	i	i	i	i	i	i	i	i	i

I created loving conditions for two women recently. I gave them middle names of Nancy and Annola, together with the single initial G. Both names are 21, which reduce to a 3, like a C, and both have two of the letter N, bringing 10 years of loving conditions during the 21 year span of the name. These women had birthdays on the 14th and 23rd. Both 14 and 23 reduce to a 5, which together with the initial N would have added unnecessary physical nerves. By giving them Nancy or Annola, it took away the need for both the C and the N as initials, but achieved a similar end result. Both of these women now have good balance in the numbers of their names and letters in their chart.

My numbers from birth were 14/22, 34/47 27/45 born on the 5th. The reduced numbers were 5/22, 7/11, 9/9 and 5. This combination has two physical nerves primary and two mental nerves in the undertone. The pendulum 22 was an undertone, making it less likely to swing as strong as a primary would, but the primary in this case was 14, which can be unpredictable, and I was. Add to this the extrovert of 14 and introvert of 27, with the undertones being extrovert 22 and introvert 45, and it made for a volatile cocktail.

When I was in positive letter combinations, I was busy, active, making money and enjoying life. The temptation to wander was not so strong. But never the less, it was always lurking in the background and waiting for an opportunity to pop up. When I was in negative letters, especially the U from my first name Paul, I went through financial problems. I can remember, looking back using my chart and saw that, these were years when my alcohol problems accelerated. The only thing keeping me on the right track, happy and pleasant around other people, was a good helping of positive letters. P, L, N, with some A's and E's coinciding at the right time to make the highs, higher. My life was literally a roller coaster until I changed my name.

I wanted to keep my strengths and lose my weaknesses. I did not dislike myself, but I disliked the way I acted at times. I could be erratic and extreme, especially when influenced by alcohol.

The numbers for my new name are 21/15, 7/2, 30/24, 50/49 and 5. The reduced numbers are 3/6, 7/2, 3/6, 5/4 and 5.

I discovered the 50 with a 49 undertone would keep some of the strengths I had from 14 and 22 and at the same time take away the unpredictable and reduce the pendulum. The 50 has physical nerves but to a much lesser degree than 14.

Obviously I was unable to change my birthday, number 5, extrovert and excess physical nerves, so I added 3/6 to tone it down. The 30 and 24 do this very well.

My numbers were 5, 5, 7, 9, 9, 11 and 22. Thank God I discovered Name Reality.

My numbers now are 2, 3, 3, 4, 5, 5 and 7.

I still have two 5's, though 50 is softer than 14. I still have one 7, but the undertone and nervous 11 is now a calm 2. The two 9's have gone and been replaced with two caring and intelligent 3's and with quiet and artistic undertone 6's. The pendulum 22 is now a slightly softer 4, (49).

The primary combination that creates my new personality is 3, 3, 5, 5, 7.

I considered adding a 1 with the 8 undertone. The numbers 10 or 28 are too extreme. I looked at number 46 with a 26 undertone. It would have been a nice to add a little more variation to the mix, but the extra activity from the 1 would not be the best choice with my birthday being a 5 and the 50 adding a touch more physical nerves. If I were twenty years old starting a new business or looking for a sports career then maybe yes, but at fifty-six, no thank you.

If you look at the vowels in Lyon G. Payley Zonamyari, you will see I have three A's, one E, one I and two O's. I do not have any U's. This is quite a good balance. The three A's do make me very active, another good reason not to add a personality that reduced to a 1, further increasing the activity. The way letters lay in the events chart is very important. I played with different name variations and eventually came up with what I have today. There are no years when the A, E, I and R fall together. Another good combination I have is the initials of each name, L.G.P.Z. My name will not appeal to everybody, but I like it and that's what is important.

I am a happy man. My life has changed in so many ways for the better. I have lost the appetite for alcohol, but I can still enjoy a glass or maybe two. Close friends confirm I am now very calm and collected with a positive attitude. Life is good!

Here is a view of my events chart. I admit, I was searching for the best possible name I could create for myself and I did focus on positive letters to help me along the way. I am happy with the result. There is nothing to hold me back or slow me down. I can achieve whatever I put my mind to within realistic boundaries.

56	57	58	59	60	61	62	63	64	65	66	67	68	69	70	71	72	73	74
o	o	n	n	n	n	n	L	L	L	y	y	y	y	y	y	y	o	o
G	G	G	G	G	G	G	G	G	G	G	G	G	G	G	G	G	G	G
y	y	y	y	P	P	P	P	P	P	P	a	y	y	y	y	y	y	y
Z	Z	o	o	o	o	o	o	n	n	n	n	n	a	m	m	m	m	y

In March of 2012, I was fortunate to meet a Catholic Anglican Priest. His name was Spencer Garnica Lever. He originates from an English speaking island in the S.W. Caribbean named San Andres. He set up a ministry in Barranquilla, Colombia some 20 years ago. His role is quite different from that of a regular man of God. He is a natural healer and works hands-on removing negative energy. You could say he is an exorcism priest and a very good one at that. He is in great demand throughout the Caribbean, Central and South America. Exorcism is a very sensitive subject which I am not qualified to try and explain. Some people will swear demons exist and many will laugh, insisting it is just a myth, good for fairy tales and movies. However, I have witnessed this man cure people from the most terrible inflictions that medical doctors could neither diagnose nor remedy.

Spencer was interested in my studies about names, so I offered to demonstrate by showing him his name. When I calculated his primary numbers, 35, 35, 26, I immediately saw the reduced numbers of 8, 8 and 8. Whilst this may be considered lucky by the Chinese, it is not for *Name Reality*. Then he told me his birthday was the 8th. I had no choice other than to inform him that he was at high risk for problems with growths, tumors or cancer of the digestive system. He said yes, you are correct. I asked why he was agreeing with me, to which he replied, "I nearly died two years ago from colon cancer." As you can imagine, I got his attention and he got mine. He had a tumor the size of a grapefruit. Doctors gave him a slim chance of surviving surgery. Spencer worked on himself, fasting and praying in seclusion for 10 days. He summonsed Angels, a technique used by many natural healers, to help reduce his tumor. When he went back to the doctors, they were amazed to see the tumor had shrunk to the size of a pea. This was subsequently removed with a simple colonoscopy procedure.

We went on to discover how his chart revealed many events throughout his early life. Most notable, was how his mid-thirties to forty-two were exceptionally good years, when he was in letters P G E. Then, on his forty-third birth day, the letters changed in his chart to E R R. This he agreed was the time when his life changed dramatically.

I explained how his future chart showed little or no improvement until his seventieth birthday, another 20 years ahead. What did concern me, were the letters for his fifty-second birthday. N N L. This is an excellent example how green positive letters can occasionally flip the opposite way and become negative. Two N's in the same year of a chart, especially one below the other, can bring double love, but often indicates health problems. The L, when in a negative chart, can indicate self-sacrifice. Needless to say, with his recent cancer scare, there was a possibility it could come back. The only good news was that at age fifty-three and fifty-four, the letters changed to C N L which indicates health recovery.

2003	2004	2005	2006	2007	2008	2009	2010	2011	2012	2013	2014	2015	2016	2017	2018	2019
41	42	43	44	45	46	47	48	49	50	51	52	53	54	55	56	57
p	p	e	e	e	e	e	n	n	n	n	n	c	c	c	e	e
G	a	r	r	r	r	r	r	r	r	r	n	n	n	n	n	i
e	e	r	r	r	r	r	r	r	r	r	L	L	L	e	e	e

I told him he had two options. Use the information like a weather forecast and prepare for a storm, or change his name.

A year later, Spencer called and said everything was exactly as I predicted. He was unable to get ahead and he did not want to go through the potential risk of cancer or tumors again. Spencer said the more he analyzed his chart, the more truths he discovered. He asked me to design him a new name. He said that his family would not speak to him if he changed his last names. I said I would do the best I could, to keep everybody happy.

The result you see here is for his new name. Anthony C. G. Ganyca Levor.

2012	2013	2014	2015	2016	2017	2018	2019	2020	2021	2022	2023	2024	2025	2026	2027	2028
50	51	52	53	54	55	56	57	58	59	60	61	62	63	64	65	66
o	o	o	o	o	o	n	n	n	n	n	y	y	y	y	y	y
C	C	C	C	C	C	C	C	C	C	C	C	C	C	C	C	C
G	G	G	G	G	G	G	G	G	G	G	G	G	G	G	G	G
G	G	G	G	G	a	n	n	n	n	n	y	y	y	y	y	y
r	r	r	r	L	L	L	e	e	e	e	e	v	v	v	v	o

Anthony C. G. Ganyca Levor. 34/29. 3/6. 7/2. 24/30. 27/27. 8. The reduced numbers are 7/11, 3/6, 7/2, 6/3, 9/9, born on the 8th. Working with people is his life, so, the 34 and 7 are a good combination. He loves the name Anthony. The C, 3/6, will give him strong health and balance nicely with the 24/30. You can find more information about Anthony on my website.

Meanwhile, if you need a man with his special skills, you can contact him at Anthony.cggl@hotmail.com

My research at the local prison has taught me how important it is to stay away from negative letter combinations in a chart when you are creating a new name. Many of the inmates had name combinations that did not trigger any serious alarm bells when I was looking at their names by numbers. I was expecting an abundance of 22's with 27's or 11's with 18's aggravated by names with more nerves, or abnormal numbers like 39, capable of murder. But this was not always the case with many of the names I analyzed. Sure, I found names with number balance problems, but the main cause was revealed when I calculated their events charts.

I discovered the biggest problems came from blue letter combinations rather than red negative letters alone. Not just one or two bad years, but several consecutive years. Many had bad letter combinations during their childhood making matters worse. Letters A, E, I and R, when together in the same year or in various configurations, often with two of the same letters doubling up, will put people into stressful overload. I cannot divulge names or information, but I can show you a couple clips from real events charts of real people in jail for serious crimes. These are letter combinations to be avoided. Even when a person has a good balance of names, these combinations will bring stressful conditions.

f	f	f	o	o	o	o	o	o	A	d	d	d	d
a	r	r	r	r	r	r	r	r	r	e	e	e	e
v	v	e	e	e	e	e	r	r	r	r	r	r	r

u	u	i	i	i	i	i	i	i	i	i	s
f	f	f	f	f	f	r	r	r	r	r	r
H	H	H	H	e	e	e	e	e	r	r	r
r	r	r	r	r	r	r	r	r	d	d	d

a	a	a	a	a	a	a	r	r	r	r	r	r	r	r	r
a	a	a	s	s	s	s	s	s	s	s	t	t	t	t	t
r	r	r	r	r	r	r	r	r	i	i	i	i	i	i	i

f	f	f	f	f	f	r	r
o	o	o	R	R	R	R	R
r	r	r	r	r	r	r	r
r	r	r	r	r	r	r	r

t	t	h	h	h	h	h	h	h	h	e	e	e	e	e	r
b	b	e	e	e	e	e	z	z	z	z	z	z	z	z	a
H	H	H	H	e	e	e	e	e	r	r	r	r	r	r	r

r	r	r	r	r	r	r	r	i	i	i
C	C	C	a	b	b	e	e	e	e	e
r	r	r	r	r	r	r	r	r	r	r

f	f	f	f	f	f	r	r	r	r	r	r	r	r
R	R	R	R	R	i	i	i	i	i	i	i	i	i
r	r	r	r	r	r	c	c	c	h	h	h	h	h
o	o	o	o	o	r	r	r	r	r	r	r	r	r

i	i	i	i	i	i	i	i
t	t	t	t	t	t	a	a
r	r	r	r	r	r	r	r
s	s	s	s	s	o	o	o

e	e	e	e	d
i	i	i	i	i
h	h	h	b	b
u	u	u	s	C

Whenever you create change or alter a name, by legal documentation, you must remember that your new name will come in as primary energy. If you are dominant in undertone and you want to keep one or more of your original names, those names will remain undertone. You will need to create an undertone chart for your original names, then cut and paste your new names from a primary chart.

If you were born undertone dominant and you create a totally new name, all the new names must be calculated as primary.

This does not apply to nicknames, even when the nickname is heavily documented, like the J in Michael J Fox. A documented nickname will continue along the same primary or undertone path you had from birth.

Positive letters in your chart are good, but it is more important to stay away from negative letter combinations. Even if there were such a thing as the perfect name and it were given to you, nothing is going to change if you sit on your butt waiting around. This is not a magical formula, so do not think you are going to win the lottery jackpot just because you have a new positive name. This is about creating a smooth road ahead allowing you to perform at your best.

A balanced positive name will give you a clear road ahead. From there, it is up to you to take advantage of this new freedom. With some careful planning, some effort and determination, within reason, you can achieve anything you put your mind to.

Changing your name requires skill, experience and a sharp eye. You must be sure the new name will benefit you for many years ahead. This book is just the beginning. With time and funding, my intention is to set up teaching programs sharing and expanding this knowledge. Meanwhile, I can be contacted through my website if you have any questions and need assistance.

www.namesdoctor.com

Chapter Sixteen

HOW TO ACTIVATE YOUR NEW NAME

Number one is documentation. You must renounce your old name and take on your new name with official documentation. If you do not, then the old names will remain and your new names will add into the mix, like a nickname or stage name as explained in previous chapters. The opening page in the last chapter gave you examples of the legal procedure in England, the USA and Colombia. You must research the rules applicable to your place of birth and the country where you live.

When you have received your important documents amended with your new name, such as passport and driver's license, you will find it very easy to change your name everywhere else. Make copies of a standard letter, showing your old and new names with a brief explanation that you have changed your name for personal reasons. You may need to have your signature on this letter witnessed or notarized. Make copies of the official document showing your legal name change, together with copies of your old and new passport or photo ID. Now make a list of everybody you can think of that has your old name documented somewhere in their files, including important institutions like banks and insurance companies. Send out this letter with copies wherever you can, by mail, email or deliver by hand.

Who you need to inform; Bank, credit card agencies, stocks/bonds/mutual funds/investments, retirement plans, all insurances, Internal Revenue Service, National Insurance or Social Security, utility companies, your employer, the post office, real estate, professional associations, your lawyer, powers of attorney, trusts, your will and other peoples wills, your doctor, your dentist, frequent flyer programs, to name a few.

The more you document your new name, the better. Using it verbally is good, but documentation is stronger. Do not worry if friends and family call you by your old name. It will cause no ill effect. Each letter in your new name represents a symbol. The combination of these symbols, create a vibration which is your new vibration. You want this new vibration to spread far and wide. Tell everybody about your new name. Not just verbally, send an email to everybody on your list. Create an email address with your new name. Try and use the full names, if not within the address then on the title that appears on inboxes. Create a header or signature with your new full names and contact numbers. Print new business cards. There are many ways to get your new name out there. You don't have to spend a lot of money doing it.

Your signature is important. Work on a new signature, including a short version and a full version. When you use your new signature, focus as you write each name and remind yourself how much you like your new name. Start or finish your signature with an underline looping up or, an underline with a dot or punctuation stop. This is another good way of expressing how your new name makes you feel good. Take pride in your new name. Love your new name. Love yourself.

While you are doing all of the above, you have to reprogram yourself, just like a computer. Your conscious and your subconscious mind know you by your old name and your old habits. Your conscious mind has already accepted your new name. It was your conscious mind that made the decision to change your name. Now you have to tell your sub conscious mind that this new name is what you want and that it is time to make some changes. Talk to yourself, it's okay, it does not mean you are going mad. Look in the bathroom mirror each morning and say with a smile on your face, *hello (your name), this is going to be another happy day.* Sing a happy song in the shower, either out loud and your day will begin on a happy note or in your mind, either way, it starts your day on a happy note. If there is a little mishap during the day, instead of aggravating yourself, laugh it off. Your subconscious mind recognizes happy and unhappy. It does not reason, it does not question. Even if you stubbed your toe and it hurt for a few seconds, laugh it off and say *silly me that was a daft thing to do. I will be more careful in future.* Say *Thank you God for allowing me to have a wonderful day,* before you go to sleep each night. This works best when you say it from your heart and when you visualize what you want within your mind.

A huge amount of information on how to improve your life is available. The more you look, the more you will find. It will not take long for you to find what works best for you.

Read, listen and watch anything that inspires you. I have already mentioned three books. *The Power of your Subconscious Mind,* by Dr. Joseph Murphy. *The Richest Man Who Ever Lived,* by Steven K Scott. *The Secret,* by Rhonda Byrne. *The Secret* lists names and websites of respected self-help motivational experts who contributed to the book. If reading is not your thing, then watch the video documentary of *The Secret.* The Internet is full of good information to reprogram your thinking. Check out another one of my favorites by going to youtube.com and search Bob Proctor, or Bob Proctor the Secret.

Make a plan for the next twelve months. Document it. Make a wish list of realistic goals you want to achieve in the next year. Make it visual. Add drawings or photographs. Put it in a place where you will see it every day. When you look at your wish list, confirm to yourself that everything is already coming. Just like you ordered an exciting new book on Amazon and you are waiting for it to arrive in your mailbox any day.

The laws of attraction are real. If your path is clear, there is nothing to stop you.

Part Three

Change the world—one baby—one name at a time.

Chapter Seventeen

CREATE A VIBRANT BALANCED NAME FOR YOUR BABY

If you are not on an e-reader and you are opening the pages of this paperback book for the first time, deliberately at this page, I have good news and I have bad news.

The good news is you are bestowed with a wonderful opportunity to give a child complete *freedom* to fulfill their God given life.

The bad news is you have to go back to the beginning of this book and read every page until you arrive back here again.

In the summer of 2012, a relative came to stay at my house with his twin boys, Thomas and Martin, aged two. *This was another personal revelation that reassured me just how incredibly good this system really is.* Obviously both boys have the same mother, father and date of birth. Neither have a middle name, so we are down to two boys who should be exactly the same except for their first names. Thomas is personality number 22 and Martin is 30. Sure enough, Thomas, with his serious expression and never content in one place, would wander all over the house, getting into everything and breaking a few things along the way. Martin was very much the opposite. He was very calm and quite happy in his room most of the time, with or without company. However, Martin's face would light up with a smile whenever his parents walked into the room. When I showed both parents the written personalities for 22 and 30, they agreed the information was extremely accurate and clearly showed the differences between the two boys. Their family name is 38, a brilliant name with high mental activity. Thomas has 22, adding more mental activity, whereas Martin, with 30, has a calming effect that compliments his 38 very well. It was clear to see then, as it is now a year later, that Thomas is extremely over active requiring a lot of attention, whereas Martin, also very bright, is very calm.

Creating the best possible name for your child is going to require some time and study, but you can be sure it will be worth every minute. If you have read all the previous pages in this book, especially Chapters Ten, Eleven, Twelve, Thirteen and Fifteen, you will already have a good idea what you need and what you don't need, to give your child the best possible start in life.

You can copy and use the work tools in Chapter Eighteen, or, for speed and accuracy, order a full set of tools via my website that you can download to your computer. The Excel program in both primary and undertone formats, calculates numbers for each name and produces a life chart with a simple click.

IMPORTANT STEPS TO FOLLOW

In every case, the baby will automatically receive the family name of the father and the maiden name of the mother. It takes the energy of two people to make a baby therefore, the baby will start its life with the vibration of both parents family names. The mother's maiden name is also documented on birth certificates in most countries. The exception is, if the mother has legally by documentation, changed her name before the birth. Marriage does not remove your maiden name, as discussed in Chapter Two. In Spain, Central and South America, it has long been tradition, that everybody has two last names or family names and women do not normally take the name of their husbands upon marriage. The two family names are therefore your starting point. Begin by calculating the numbers for both of these names and study the personalities.

Check to see if the two family names balance or conflict numerically. Prepare an events chart with just the two names to see if there are any years with negative letter combinations. Be very careful with the letter combinations for the first few years of the baby's life regarding health. B, for example, is sensitive towards health if mixed with W worry or, H stress, T the brain is aggravated by E for extreme. It is good to avoid letters doubling up in the same year like B, D, L, M, N, R and T. Use powerful positive letters where you can such as, C, G, J, K, L, N, P, Q, Y and Z within names or as single initials, especially C, G, N and Y.

Two names with physical or mental nerves are going to put you at the maximum, leaving no tolerance for another name with nervous energy. If you have two family names with nervous energy, you need to balance this with a first name number that produces a calming effect. Refer to the second page of Chapter Ten. You can also give the child two or even three names, to reduce the size of each slice from the cake, as referred to in the fourth page of Chapter Ten.

If the two family names clash heavily by numbers and have poor letter combinations in the events chart, there is an option. As I write this very chapter, my daughter is seven months into her pregnancy. Her family name is 27 and the father's family name is 22, an extremely volatile combination of numbers. The letters from both names, when combined in a chart, do not bring any bright prospects for the forthcoming baby. To combat this, my daughter is legally changing her name, so when the baby is born it does not receive any influence from the 27. This might seem drastic until you fully understand the power of names and the way they can influence life.

There is an upside. My daughter is changing her last name to that of her fiancée. It was their intention to marry and for her to take his name upon marriage some months ago but issues beyond their control have delayed the wedding. When the family name of the mother and father are the same, like Smith and Smith, the baby will only receive the energy one time. Problem solved. Now, we can continue creating a good name for my daughter's baby and yours too.

Make a list of your preferred names. There are numerous websites or books with thousands of names listed in alphabetical order. Calculate the numbers for these names and check to see if the numbers balance or clash with the two family names. If a name you really like does not balance by number try changing the spelling, preferably by using positive letters to alter the numerical addition until it does balance, if not, you have to start over. Begin adding names of your choice to the charts and see how the letters appear across the years. This is a process of elimination. It can take time, but you can make it fun.

While doing this, do not forget the undertones. It is highly likely that your baby will be born dominant in primary like the majority of the population. However, you must run the same checks in case your baby is born undertone dominant.

When you have come down to a short list of favorite names that balance with the family names, do the cross reference. The undertone numbers will now be the ones that create the personality of your baby. This can paint a very different picture. If you have a good helping of positive letters within all the names for your proposed baby's name, the events chart will change, but not usually for the worse. Again, this is a process of elimination. If at first you do not succeed, do try again.

My research with an astrologer tells me that undertones can be linked to your birth date, birth time and place of birth. More specifically, the balance in your elements; earth, water, air and fire. I hope that soon we will be able to tell you by an astrological reading if you or your baby is primary or undertone dominant. Until such research is complete, continue with the same method of cross checking primary and undertone calculations.

The wild card is going to be the date of birth. As you have seen from the previous chapters, one number can make a big difference. If you have an indication as to your child's birth date, you can play with numbers around this date and create a safe set of names/numbers if the fixed family names allow you to do so. Not an easy task and very disappointing if the baby arrives early or late. Many mothers today are opting for a C-section birth, sometimes with a pre-arranged date close to the expected time of birth. In some countries like China, the superstition with numbers is so crazy that some couples are insisting upon a C-section birth on a specific pre-arranged date, sometimes to an exact hour!

This is a decision only you can make. You can have a backup name ready if the birth date is not what you expected. Or, you can leave it in the hands of our Creator. Depending upon the rules that apply in your country of residence, you may be able to change your baby's name soon after birth. This gives you the ability to work with a clean slate and create whatever you please based around one fixed number, which is a very special number, your child's birth day.

The Social Security Administration in the United States announced the 2012 most popular baby names on its website. The top 10, with the appropriate *Name Reality* numbers calculated are:

Girls	Boys
Sophia. 32/31	Jacob. 13/32
Emma. 14/22	Mason. 17/28
Isabella. 25/56	Ethan. 21/24
Olivia. 32/40	Noah. 20/16
Ava. 6/21	William. 34/47
Emily. 28/26	Liam. 17/28
Abigail. 32/49	Jayden. 23/31
Madison. 30/42	Michael. 33/39
Elizabeth. 43/47	Alexander. 39/51
Mia. 14/22	Aiden. 24/30

Liam is a new entry to the top 10, making the list for the first time. An Irish short form of William, Liam didn't enter the U.S. top 1,000 until 1967. Its popularity has been spurred by celebrity Liam Neeson. Liam replaces Daniel, 27/36.

Elizabeth climbed back onto the girls' top 10, unseating Chloe.

Here are the top 10 most searched baby girl names for 2013:

Isabella, 25/56
Millie, 33/39
Sookie, 29/34
Ann, 11/16
Ella, 12/24
Betty, 18/27
Ellie, 25/29
Emma, 14/22
Eithne, 34/29
Charlotte, 39/51

The top 10 most searched baby boy names for 2013:

Jacob, 13/32
Max, 11/16
Liam, 17/28
Ted, 11/16
Mo, 10/8
Aiden, 24/30
Andy, 17/19
Bertie, 32/40
Ned, 13/14
Gus, 11/16

More names with ready-made calculations can be found on my website www.namesdoctor.com

Last but not least.

Chapter Eighteen

WORK TOOLS

Primary Numbers Chart

1	2	3	4	5	6	7	8	9
A	B	C	D	E	F	G	H	I
J	K	L	M	N	O	P	Q	R
S	T	U	V	W	X	Y	Z	#

Undertone Numbers Chart

9	8	7	6	5	4	3	2	1
#	A	B	C	D	E	F	G	H
I	J	K	L	M	N	O	P	Q
R	S	T	U	V	W	X	Y	Z

0	1	2	3	4	5	6	7	8	9	10	11	12	13	14	15	16	17	18	19

20	21	22	23	24	25	26	27	28	29	30	31	32	33	34	35	36	37	38	39

40	41	42	43	44	45	46	47	48	49	50	51	52	53	54	55	56	57	58	59

60	61	62	63	64	65	66	67	68	69	70	71	72	73	74	75	76	77	78	79

80	81	82	83	84	85	86	87	88	89	90	91	92	93	94	95	96	97	98	99

Blank Chart 10 lines deep.

Name Reality

Green letters are Positive. Red letters are usually Negative.

Blue Letters are influenced by other letters.

Green letters can bring out the Positive in Blue.

Red letters can bring out the Negative in Blue.

A: Adds activity to all other letters.

B: Intuitive, sensitive or highly strung. Stress=illness. N= marriage. Beware 2xB health.

C: Control, strong health with the ability to cope. Very Positive.

D: Change, expansion, more responsibility. Travel. Beware 2xD accidents.

E: Extremes. Good things Better. Bad things Worse.

F: Concealment by you or towards you. To discover, search and find.

G: Gains in all areas. Very Positive.

H: Stress and Strain. Not always negative, can be strain or striving for gain.

I: Exaggerates Emotions. Highs and lows.

J: Leadership in Family or Career.

K: Change. Travel. Strong health. Period of Learning. Apprehension when negative.

L: Change Advancement Travel. Beware 2xL accidents, self-sacrifice.

M: Change Travel Beware 2xM can be dangerous.

N: Love and Romantic Conditions. Very Positive Sometimes 2xN indicates health.

O: Money and Stability. Beware 2xO health or very slow.

P: Power and Success but beware of spending.

Q: Very Positive for Career Health and Travel.

R: Busy Active Rushing around Beware 2xR = overactive/accidents/illness/family.

S: Sharpens for better or worse but improves.

T: Home or Career Change Beware 2xT head area.

U: Losses—Financial, Emotional or Health. Can be very negative.

V: Can weaken your character, but often brings travel.

W: Wavering conditions. Anxiety Worry Self-doubts. Travel in a good table.

X: Clumsy or accident prone. Very dependent upon other letters in the chart.

Y: Success in all areas. Very Positive.

Z: Controls and Represses. Promotes your people skills.

Chapter Nineteen

ROAD OF DISCOVERY

The more you study this system, the more you can discover about the human race and the behavior people display. During my first year of study back in 2010, when I ran out of friends' names and family members' names to analyze, I would analyze any name that came up in the news, trying to find a link. I studied success stories like Rihanna who benefitted with double Y's in her names: Robyn and Fenty. I saw Simon Cowell enjoying 14 years of back to back P's from his middle name Phillip and a great deal of success. These are two examples you saw in chapter fourteen. Unfortunately, the news is not always hyping success stories. I found just as many truths while analyzing the names of people who committed terrible acts.

My first breakthrough was getting my hands on a copy of Veolita's book in 2011. This took me to a new level. The works of Veolita and Evrita Parke Boyle can be traced back well before 1929. They were actively researching different systems before settling on what I have titled, *Name Reality.* However little seems to exist after their last publication in 1934. The Second World War was about to start, which may have had something to do with the trail ending. Does anybody know of living relatives or what became of them? If so, please contact me.

If you read their book, or more specifically the sixty-four personalities, you will see each number is split into three parts. The first is a general overview in English. The second is called the Hebrew Cabbala, but translated into comprehendible English. The third part, called The Chinese Tao and Yi-King, has been translated word for word into English, but is not always comprehendible. Let me give you an example. *Dimunition and increase. Overflowing and emptiness. Should be employed in sacrifice. The violent or strong do not die a natural death.* A large amount of text is written this way. I can only assume there were secrets Veolita and Elvrita were not quite ready to divulge back in 1929 to an apprehensive audience.

This brings me to my second breakthrough. I am most fortunate that my spiritual mentor, a lady of Japanese and English decent, happens to be quite an expert at making sense of these phrases. She has incredible talent for many other subjects too. Her interpretations of the Chinese Tao and Yi-King have enabled me to complete the information you see for the sixty-four personalities. I believe Veolita and Elvrita would approve.

To be honest, I have breakthroughs every week, sometimes daily. Many are little discoveries, but they make me happy and keep me searching for more.

In the summer of 2012, a relative came to stay at my house with his twin boys, Thomas and Martin, aged two. This was another personal revelation that reassured me just how incredibly good this system really is. I mentioned this story in the first page of Chapter Seventeen, outlining the remarkable differences between these twins, clearly shown by their personality numbers.

My research since January 2013 has gone much deeper. I ran out of celebrities to analyze so I went to the local Alcoholics Anonymous. I had no problem relating to the people there because I was one of them before I changed my name. However, I found exactly what I expected and more. With time, a lot more can be done with names relating to addiction problems. I have worked with Dr. Tito Palacio, confirming and sometimes adding new information to his professional assessments for patients with physical or re-occurring psychological problems.

My most exciting project to date, has been analyzing the names of serious offenders at the local jail. The prison warden was very impressed with the accuracy of *Name Reality* and granted me access once a week to enter the jail. I have been studying the names of serious offenders, making my confidential report and then discussing the evaluations with the senior staff. We are currently looking at the option of name change for some of the inmates who want to reform and improve their lives. Two have already volunteered and I expect more to follow.

I have recently discovered that sex-a-holics have the same personality number combinations. I frequently see medical conditions with re-occurring name or letter combinations. I am not saying names are the cause or cure. However, there are strong indications that some names can aggravate specific medical conditions, such as bi-polar or manic depressive disorders. Therefore, it is not unrealistic to assume that a name change could assist and aid recovery. There could be a link to children and adults with Attention Deficit Disorder. More answers can be found with time, study and research.

There is so much more to learn about people and the affects created by names. The A to Z alphabet is just one language interpreted by symbols. This system was used in China, though obviously not with letters A to Z. There is no reason why it cannot be converted back to relate to Chinese, or any other language. I am just one person, limited to the hours in a day. With more research, great discoveries can be made. Until such time when a development program can be put in place, I will continue to change the world, one name at a time.

I will keep you informed with information and new discoveries on my website.

www.namesdoctor.com

Chapter Twenty

TRIBUTE TO THE LADIES OF NAMES

There is nothing more important or fascinating to each individual than his or her own personal life. Any one desiring to become a musician must not only have a thorough knowledge of music, but also a thorough knowledge of the instrument he has decided to master. There are many people who have no desire to master any musical instrument of the ordinary type, but there is not one human being who would not master his own individual life if he could.

You are a musical instrument. Your body and the conditions of your life are the result of the harmonies or discords played by you or upon you from day to day, by your own personal name.

It is bringing you good, or it is bringing you harm. It is bringing you strength or it is bringing you weakness. You can name your children for success or failure. You can name your children for health or illness.

You can understand these and a hundred more by having knowledge of the Chinese Sacred Science of Vibration.

The object of this book is to call the attention of seriously intelligent people to a great science involving the fundamental principles of the universe. A knowledge which until recently has been closed to the average man in the western world. Its true department is among the vibratory forces of physics, in the same category as Internet, television, radio, music, atmospheric waves and lines of similar order. This is where it will finally be placed when, like many other science, it has sounded the gamut of skeptical unbelief and the bad handling of un-scientific people

These are the words of Veolita and Elvrita Parke Boyle, from their book; *The Fundamental Principles of the Yi-King, Tao; The Cabbalas of Egypt and the Hebrews*, published in 1929. Without the passion and relentless study of these two women, my book would not exist today.

I thank the team at Telemachus, especially author advisor Joanne Lewis, whose professional responsive support made self-publishing this book incredibly easy. I would like to thank my daughter Gemma for introducing me to Laurence Payg. I would like to thank Laurence for his many long conversations and for sharing his experiences gained over the years as a name analyst.

Eventually we all find our way, if not in this life then maybe in the next.

I hope this book helps guide you to achieve health and happiness.

Lyon G. Payley Zonamyari

Lightning Source UK Ltd.
Milton Keynes UK
UKOW06f1427010615

252680UK00011B/115/P

9 781939 927743